WE DON'T HAVE A CTE PROBLEM... WE HAVE A PERCEPTION PROBLEM

PERCEPTION SHIFT™

HOW EDUCATION LEADERS CHANGE THE NARRATIVE
SO STUDENTS CHOOSE CAREER AND TECHNICAL EDUCATION
AND COMMUNITIES BELIEVE IN IT

DR. DONNA PRUDHOMME

2026 ACTE NATIONAL ADMINISTRATOR OF THE YEAR
2025 ACTE REGION IV ADMINISTRATOR OF THE YEAR | 2024 CTAT TEXAS ADMINISTRATOR OF THE YEAR

Disclaimer

The author is not a lawyer. For legal advice, please seek an attorney as the contents of this book should not be construed as legal advice in any way. Every effort has been made to ensure the accuracy of the information within this book. However, we cannot be held liable for any omissions, errors, or inconsistencies. You are solely responsible for actions taken (or not taken) based on the information contained in this book.

Printed in the United States of America

ISBN: 978-1-7331188-8-0

www.drdonnaprudhomme.com

speak@drdonnaprudhomme.com

DR. DONNA PRUDHOMME

DEDICATION

This book is dedicated to my beloved sister, Nasheka Lasha Powell, affectionately known as Shay. Your presence is deeply missed every day, but I feel your spirit guiding me on this journey. You were one of the biggest cheerleaders for the people you loved—always present, always proud, always pushing us forward. This work, and the belief that our stories deserve to be told, is for you.

IN MEMORY OF

NASHEKA LASHA POWELL "SHAY"

April 17, 1980—July 18, 2020

Nasheka was always a hard worker and strived to be the best in everything she pursued. She was an honor student and graduated from West Brook High School in 1998. After graduation, she continued her education at Lamar University, where she received a Bachelor of Science in Marketing and a Master of Business Administration from Regent University.

Nasheka joined the Centers for Disease Control and Prevention in 2007 as a health communications specialist in the National Center for Health Marketing. She provided executive communication support for Center leaders and led the health marketing podcast series. She was recognized as CDC Employee of the Month and received a nomination for a Daytime Emmy Award for a project she led with Georgia Public Broadcasting. One of her most visible contributions was her leadership in the successful development and installation of a permanent exhibit within the David J. Sencer CDC Museum—a contribution that required a mix of creativity, skill, and sheer persistence to complete. At the CDC, it was her approach to work that made her so special and treasured. She was a generous, kind, and consummate colleague capable of leading and following without ego. Her smile and genuine warmth inspired and encouraged all around her.

Always a faithful servant, Nasheka started a prayer call ministry known as Purpose Under Fire—a simple reminder that our help comes from the Lord. She believed that in the midst of whatever life is throwing your way, you should release it to God and remind yourself of who He is. You do not have to worry. You do not have to second guess. He specializes in carrying the weight, the burden, and the pressures of life for you. She believed that God's got you. He will help and strengthen you. There is no one like the Lord.

In honor of her legacy, the Purpose Under Fire Scholarship Fund has been established in her name. Nasheka was a sweet, loving woman with a beautiful smile—always willing to help and sacrifice for others. A praying woman who loved unconditionally. Her endless faith in God, her kindness, and her strength will continue to live on.

To everything she was.
To everything she gave.
To everything she believed.

ACKNOWLEDGEMENTS

First and foremost, I want to thank God for the opportunity to serve students, to lead with purpose, and to use my voice on behalf of Career and Technical Education. This work has always felt like a calling, and I am grateful for the platform and the persistence to see it through. There were moments in this journey when I could not see the full picture—when the resistance was heavy, when the recognition had not yet come, when I was fighting for a seat at a table that did not always feel ready to receive me. But I held on to the promise that has carried me through every season of this work: "For I know the plans I have for you, declares the LORD, plans to prosper you and not to harm you, plans to give you hope and a future" (Jeremiah 29:11 NIV). That promise was not just for me. It was for every student who needed someone to believe in their pathway before they believed in it themselves. And it was for this work—which was always bigger than one person, one district, or one award.

To my husband, Michael: Your unwavering support has been the cornerstone of everything I have built. You witnessed my exhaustion, the long nights, the challenges, and the moments of doubt, and you never once told me to give up. I still hear your voice saying, "You are always working hard, and eventually, something will happen." You were right. Your belief in me has been a constant source of strength, and this book would not exist without you.

To my son, Jay: Watching you navigate every barrier, stay focused through every disruption, and arrive at exactly where you were always meant to be has reminded me every day why this work matters. You're the reason I tell the story. I'm so proud of who you are and who you're becoming.

To my daughter, Brielle: Watching you build your brand and walk through doors that most people spend years reaching for has filled me with a pride that words can't fully hold. You're a living example of what this book is about, and you didn't even know it.

To my sisters, Yvonne Powell Cooper and Shawna Powell Gaines: Both of you have been there for me my entire life. Yvonne, the leader—never letting me lose direction, always preaching the truth, and providing encouragement when I needed it most. Shawna, the protector—always on call, never letting anyone or anything get in my way. We've lost a piece of ourselves in Nasheka. The pain of no longer having her at our sister gatherings, no longer hearing her laugh, and no longer seeing that beautiful smile is something no amount of time can truly heal. This unbearable pain has brought us closer together even though we still don't fully understand why she left us so soon. We have stood on what our parents raised us to believe—that God knows best. Watching our children grow up together and our family bond deepen over the years always reminds me of who we are and who we'll always be. We are—and will always be—"POWELLFUL."

To my CTE team (Alicia Green, Eva LeBlanc, LaChandra Cobb-Eaglin, Shamine Cormier, Tanya Anderson, and Stephanie Donald): You are the reason the work moved. You showed up every day believing in students who did not yet believe in themselves, celebrating pathways that the system had not yet fully honored, and telling the CTE story long before the world was fully ready to hear it. This book belongs to you as much as it belongs to me. It is important to have the right people at your table—and I have been blessed to have the very best.

To Dr. Shannon Allen, my former superintendent: Thank you for being a great boss, mentor, and friend. Your leadership created the space for this work to grow, and your presence at the table sent a message to everyone watching that CTE matters at the highest level. I am grateful for you.

To my colleagues who saw something in this work worth nominating, worth recognizing, and worth celebrating at every level, from district to region to national: Thank you for believing in the story before the world did.

And to every CTE student, teacher, counselor, and leader who has ever fought to be seen, heard, and valued: This book is for you. You were never the problem. You were always the answer. Keep speaking. Keep building. Keep telling your story.

TABLE OF CONTENTS

PART 03: OWNERSHIP & AWARENESS

The Story Behind the Shift

PART 04: SHIFTING THE NARRATIVE

P — Prioritize Access and Equity | T — Train the Influencers

PART 05: LEADING THE SYSTEM SHIFT

I — Integrate the Message | O — Own the Narrative

PART 06: NORMALIZING CTE

N — Normalize CTE as a First Choice

APPENDIX

FOREWORD

DR. SHANNON ALLEN

Former Superintendent of Schools, Beaumont Independent School District

It is my honor to introduce this book and the remarkable leader who wrote it. Dr. Donna Prudhomme has served as the director of Career and Technical Education for Beaumont Independent School District for the past eight years. In that time, I have had a front-row seat to one of the most intentional and impactful transformations in CTE that I have witnessed in my career as an educator. With over twenty-eight years of experience in education, Dr. Prudhomme brings a rare and comprehensive perspective to this work—and this book is the fullest expression of everything she has built, believed, and fought for.

Dr. Prudhomme is a passionate, creative, and innovative leader who continually puts her unique stamp on the CTE program. Under her leadership, CTE in Beaumont ISD has experienced significant growth and evolution. Her dedication to creating opportunities for students is evident in her work to introduce CTE programming as early as pre-K, exposing students to a wide variety of fields and igniting their interest long before they enter high school.

One of Dr. Prudhomme's greatest strengths is her ability to think outside the box, bringing innovative ideas to life that engage not only students but also the community. Her team's road shows are a prime example of this creative approach—allowing young students to explore different CTE pathways and learn about careers they may not have considered otherwise. Under her leadership, the expansion of community partnerships has resulted in local businesses offering internships and hands-on learning experiences for high school students, further enhancing the relevance and real-world application of their studies.

One of Dr. Prudhomme's signature initiatives is the CTE Choice Awards. This annual event celebrates the achievements of both students and teachers in the CTE program. It is a memorable and exciting occasion with a red-carpet atmosphere, Grammy-style announcers, and meaningful recognition for students who earn industry-based certifications and other career and technical awards. Due to its popularity, the event has outgrown several venues, and Dr. Prudhomme's team has had to secure one of the largest venues in the city to accommodate the growing number of attendees. Both students and families feel privileged to be a part of this special event.

Her outstanding leadership was recognized at the national level when she was named the 2026 Association for Career and Technical Education (ACTE) Administrator of the Year. She has also earned recognition as the 2025 ACTE Region IV Administrator of the Year and the 2024 Career and Technical Association of Texas (CTAT) Administrator of the Year. These honors are a testament to her vision, dedication, and tireless efforts in advancing Career and Technical Education and ensuring that students have access to high-quality programs that prepare them for future careers.

Dr. Prudhomme's tireless commitment to her students, her innovative thinking, and her ability to build strong community connections make her an exceptional leader in CTE. I have no doubt that her contributions to education will continue to have a profound impact on the lives of students in Beaumont ISD and beyond for many years to come.

What you are holding in your hands is more than a book about Career and Technical Education. It is a leadership blueprint, a personal testimony, and a call to action. It is the story of what happens when one leader decides that the problem is not the program—it is the perception. And it is proof that when you own that truth, everything begins to change.

I am privileged to work alongside Dr. Prudhomme. And I am proud to recommend this book to every education leader who is ready to do the same.

INTRODUCTION

WE DON'T HAVE A CTE PROBLEM—WE HAVE A PERCEPTION PROBLEM

Somewhere right now, a student is being directed away from Career and Technical Education. Not because CTE isn't a good fit. Not because the program lacks rigor or relevance. But because somewhere along the way—in the hallways, in the headlines, at the kitchen table, in the silence of what nobody says out loud—a story was told. And that story said CTE is for students who can't do anything else.

That student deserves better. And so do you.

I have spent years inside this work—as a CTE teacher, an elementary and high school counselor, a high school assistant principal and magnet school coordinator, a high school principal, and a director of CTE who has watched outstanding programs go unseen, under-chosen, and underfunded. Not because they weren't good but because nobody believed they were. Not enough parents. Not enough counselors. Not enough community members—the ones sitting in boardrooms making decisions that shape our students' futures—believed in what CTE could offer.

As a published author of books and planners designed to help students plan their futures from pre-K through adulthood, I've spent my career on both sides of this work—in the classroom and at the table where decisions are made. This book is the intersection of both.

Here's what I know to be true: CTE is not the problem. Perception is. And perception, unlike funding formulas or legislative calendars, is something education leaders can actually change.

We don't have a CTE problem.
We have a perception problem.

This book was written by someone who has lived it. I've seen students choose programs beneath their potential because no one told them CTE was their potential. I've watched gifted CTE teachers pour themselves into courses that were quietly treated as just an elective in the worst sense of the word—optional, peripheral, and easy to cut. I've sat in district meetings where CTE was the last item on the agenda, if it made the agenda, and the first thing removed when time ran short.

And I've watched what happens when leaders decide to change the narrative. Enrollment increases. Community partners show up. Parents stop asking "But what about college?" and start asking "How do I get my child into this program?" Students who once slipped through the cracks find a pathway that sees them, and they rise to meet it. That transformation doesn't begin with a new program. It begins with a new story.

At the center of this work is the P.E.R.C.E.P.T.I.O.N. Shift™, a leadership framework designed to help education leaders intentionally change how Career and Technical Education is positioned and understood. This framework isn't about quick fixes or temporary strategies. It's about sustained, thoughtful leadership that aligns messaging, access, visibility, and belief.

As you move through this book, you'll examine the narratives that have shaped CTE over time, the influences that guide student and parent decision-making, and the internal beliefs that impact how educators present pathways to students. More importantly, you'll be challenged to reflect on your own role in shaping perception—not as a point of blame but as a point of empowerment. Because the moment we acknowledge that perception is the issue is the moment we recognize that it's also something we have the ability to change. The perception gap will not close itself. It closes one leader at a time—one decision, one conversation, one celebration at a time.

Career and Technical Education holds immense potential to create access, opportunity, and economic mobility for students. But its full impact can only be realized when it's fully believed in. That's the work ahead. Not improving what's already strong but elevating how it's seen.

When we stop treating CTE as just an elective,
the perception will change.

—DR. DONNA PRUDHOMME

PART

01

POSITIONING THE TRUTH

P — Position the Truth | E — Examine the Current Narrative | R — Reveal the Hidden Messages

CHAPTER 1

THE CTE PROBLEM THAT ISN'T A PROBLEM

CTE is strong—so why does it still feel undervalued?

Career and Technical Education doesn't have a quality problem. In fact, in many districts across the country, CTE programs are stronger than they've ever been. Students are earning industry-based certifications, participating in work-based learning experiences, and graduating with skills that position them for both college and careers. From health science to manufacturing, from information technology to business, marketing, and real estate, CTE has evolved into something far more rigorous, relevant, and impactful than it was decades ago.

In my own district, I've seen this strength firsthand. I've watched students earn industry-based certifications that position them for immediate employment upon graduation. I've witnessed partnerships with industry that create opportunities many students wouldn't otherwise have access to. We tied the state of Texas in industry-based certifications and then surpassed them in Level 1 certifications. An industry-based certification (IBC) is a credential recognized by business and industry at the local, state, or national level. It isn't a classroom grade. It isn't a participation award. It's an assessment, examination, license, or training administered by the same industries that are actively hiring. A student who earns an IBC has demonstrated mastery of a specific skill set that employers value and recognize. A Level 1 certificate is a postsecondary credential—college-level work completed while still in high school, often through dual enrollment with a community college or technical institute. These aren't soft credentials. They're the kind of qualifications that open doors to employment, advanced training, and career pathways before a student ever walks across a graduation stage. That level of achievement doesn't happen by chance. It happens when programs are intentional, when expectations are high, and when students are given access to meaningful opportunities.

Career and Technical Education is designed around one promise—preparing students for high-demand, high-skill, and high-wage careers. Not someday. Not eventually.

The numbers in our own district tell the story clearly. In the 2024–2025 school year, 3,104 students were enrolled in CTE courses—with 2,962 of those students in grades 9 through 12. Our CTE completion rate reached 51.8 percent, meaning more than half of our CTE students completed a full program of study, including at least one Level 3 or Level 4 course. We offer 22 programs of study across 12 career cluster pathways, delivered by 77 dedicated CTE teachers. These aren't small numbers. These aren't the numbers of a department that's struggling. These are the numbers of a department that's producing—consistently, intentionally, and at a level that the data confirms. The programs are strong. The students are committed. The outcomes are real.

And yet, the perception hasn't always reflected what the numbers show. Despite all this progress, something still doesn't align. CTE still feels undervalued. It still feels like something that has to be explained, justified, or promoted in ways that other programs do not. If something is truly strong, it shouldn't require constant explanation. But CTE does. And that's where the real problem begins.

> ***The problem is not what CTE offers. The problem is what people believe it offers.***

I remember one of my earliest experiences with perception long before I became director of CTE, before I had language for what I was seeing. I was a CTE teacher at my high school alma mater, West Brook High School—teaching criminal justice at the same school where, eight years earlier, I had walked the halls as a student full of promise. This was the place where I'd been told I could be anything and everything I wanted to be. Being back there as a professional felt full circle.

One day, I walked into the front office to bring my supply order to the principal's secretary. It was a normal day, nothing significant about it. I needed scissors, file folders, and ink pens. Just supplies for my classroom. As I stood there, a senior English teacher looked at me and said, very casually, "You think you're important." There was no build-up. No explanation. Just that statement. For a moment, I stood still—not because I believed it but because of how quickly something so significant had been said so casually. Before I could even process it fully, the principal's secretary, Selwyn Jones, looked directly at her and said: "She *is* important."

That moment has stayed with me for my entire career. Not because of the comment itself but because of what it revealed. All I had wanted to do was place a supply order. And because I was a CTE teacher making that request, I was being positioned as less than. Less than the English teacher standing next to me. Less than worthy of the basic supplies I needed to do my job. The message was not spoken in those exact words, but it was received with perfect clarity: Your work matters less. Value can be assigned—or taken away—in an instant. And often, it isn't based on truth. It's based on perception.

Years later, I realized that Career and Technical Education was still experiencing the same thing every single day. As I moved through different roles in education—CTE teacher, elementary and high school counselor, high school assistant principal and magnet school coordinator, high school principal, and eventually director of CTE—I began to see that same dynamic play out in subtle, consistent patterns. Career and Technical Education was strong. But it wasn't seen that way.

When I was a high school counselor, I experienced this firsthand. There was a strong stigma attached to the CTE Center. It was widely believed—by students and sometimes even staff—that only special education students attended those programs. That belief wasn't written anywhere. It wasn't formally taught. But it existed, and it influenced decisions. I found myself in conversation after conversation with students who would dismiss the CTE Center before they even understood what it offered. They had already decided what it meant to attend there. I would sit with them, explain the programs, walk them through the opportunities. But I quickly realized I wasn't just providing information. I was trying to shift a belief. And that's a much more difficult task.

During my son's sophomore year, I remember asking my son why he didn't come to the career center presentation, and I will never forget what he told me. He said that one of his AP teachers had told the class they didn't need to attend because they were "too smart" to go there, and she kept her students in class instead. The most concerning part was not that it was said. It was that it was believed. That's how perception works—it doesn't need to be repeated constantly. It only needs to be reinforced enough times that it begins to feel true.

At the same time, I saw the other side of this through my son's journey. And this is a story I have to tell fully because it's the reason I do this work.

My husband and I always knew he had a passion for designing and building things. From a very young age, he was fascinated by cars. Before he could even pronounce their names correctly, he could identify every make and model by its emblem alone. He would flip through the Yellow Pages in the telephone book and match the logos to the cars we drove. His dad bought him a Hot Wheels car every trip to Walmart, and before long, he had a collection that filled an entire room—what he called his "bye-bye cars." He did not just collect them. He studied them. He would line them up on his *Cars* Lightning McQueen race rug and analyze every detail, every curve, every feature. That same intensity carried into building blocks. He built cars, robots, houses—his hands always seemed to know what his future would require. I watched all of this, and I knew with the certainty that only a mother who has been paying close attention can know that this child was going to spend his life designing, building, or engineering something.

That passion grew with him. In tenth grade, he took an engineering course—the exact pathway that aligned with who he'd always been. But in his eleventh-grade year, the engineering program was moved to another campus, a barrier that quietly redirects many students away from the paths they were building toward. He didn't let that stop him—and neither did I. As his mother, I made sure he participated in engineering activities outside of school, because sometimes the most important CTE advocacy happens at your own kitchen table. He was a dual-credit and fine arts student who had started playing tenor saxophone in middle school and went on to become drum major his junior and senior year. He carried multiple identities at once, the way students do when we actually let them. There was no us versus them, no fine arts versus CTE. Both lived in him simultaneously. And through all of it, he never let go of his passion for design and engineering.

Then came COVID-19, and with it, a series of losses that no timeline could have prepared our family for.

His senior year was interrupted in ways none of us could have anticipated. The milestones he had worked toward—senior prom, senior picnic, senior skip day, senior trip, graduation—were cancelled or transformed into drive-by parades and socially distanced outdoor ceremonies, governed by COVID-19 guidelines. The graduation ceremonies happened, but the feeling of them was different. His graduation ceremony was divided by alphabets A–K in the morning and L–Z in the evening and was held outdoors at the football stadium. He was heartbroken, and this pain and disappointment was nothing that a mother could fix. I told him something then that I meant with my whole heart: If I could give him the final months of my senior year, I would, and that one day, he will be able to tell his children that he was part of history. He did not fully understand it at the time. But I believe he will one day.

What made that season even heavier was the grief our family was already carrying. He had lost his grandfather in 2014, his grandmother in 2015. Those were my parents. Then, in July 2020—just two months after COVID-19 closed his senior year—he lost his aunt, my younger sister, one of his biggest cheerleaders, whom he loved deeply and who had been very close to him his entire life. He was navigating a disrupted senior year, Hurricane Harvey, Tropical Storm Imelda, a global pandemic, and profound personal loss, all at the same time. And yet, he kept moving.

He enrolled at Lamar University, ranked among the top engineering colleges in Texas, as a mechanical engineering major. The road was not smooth. Thermodynamics II and his work schedule never quite got along. There were semesters when he questioned whether he was capable, whether the path was still his, whether he should transfer and continue somewhere else. Internship applications went unanswered through his sophomore and junior years. There were moments when giving up would've been the easier choice. At times, as a mother, you know when your child is not happy, and many days he wasn't. And it broke my heart because I knew that everything he had carried from such a young age was a heavy burden for him to bear.

He didn't give up. I made sure he always knew he didn't have to face it alone.

The doors started opening. Internships came. Interviews followed. And then, on Friday, December 12, 2025, I captured a moment I will carry for the rest of my life. At his college graduation ceremony, before he had walked across the stage to receive his mechanical engineering degree, my son received a phone call. The one that changes everything. The one that confirmed every sacrifice, every disruption, and every hard season had been worth it. A job offer at the largest oil refinery in the United States and one of the largest in the world. He looked at me with the biggest smile I have ever seen on his face. And I broke down in tears, not because I was surprised but because I had watched every single step of that journey. The Hot Wheels cars. The building blocks. The Yellow Pages. The tenor saxophone. The drum major whistles. The COVID-19 disruption. The hurricane and tropical storm. The grief. The years of punching a clock and chasing a degree at the same time. The unanswered applications. The moments when he probably wanted to quit. And through every single one of those steps, with faith and prayer, I had believed he would arrive exactly where he did. This is what every mother wants for their child: for them to make it and to live a better life than they did.

That image—my son, his smile, that phone call—represents everything Career and Technical Education is designed to do. It connects education to passion. It connects passion to preparation. And it connects preparation to opportunity in a way that is direct, real, and life-changing. That's what CTE does when we let it. That's what CTE does when we believe in it.

But not every student pushes through barriers like that. Many make decisions earlier, based not on what is possible but on what is perceived. We can provide access all day long. We can build programs, create pathways, and open doors. But if students don't believe those doors lead somewhere meaningful, they won't walk through them.

The moment I fully understood this, my focus shifted. I stopped asking "How do we get more students into CTE?" and started asking "How do we change what students believe about CTE before they ever make a decision?"

That question changed everything because it moved the work from programs to perception. From offerings to understanding. From access to belief. This is where the shift begins. Not with adding more programs, not with providing more information, but with intentionally changing how Career and Technical Education is seen, understood, and valued. Because once perception changes, everything else follows. Students choose differently. Parents respond differently. Educators speak differently. And systems begin to align in ways they never have before.

We don't have a CTE problem. We have a perception problem. And now that we can see it clearly, we have no excuse not to change it.

CHAPTER 2

HOW WE ACCIDENTALLY CREATED THE PERCEPTION

Systems, structures, and messaging over time

The perception of Career and Technical Education did not happen overnight. It was not created by a single decision, a single policy, or a single group of people. Instead, it developed gradually over time, shaped by systems, structures, and messaging that, while well-intentioned, collectively influenced how CTE is seen today. No one set out to create a perception problem. In fact, most of the decisions that contributed to it were made with the goal of expanding opportunities for students.

When I reflect on my journey in education starting in 1998, I recognize that while many things changed, one thing remained surprisingly consistent. The perception of Career and Technical Education had not evolved. Programs improved. Opportunities expanded. Industry partnerships strengthened. But the way people thought about CTE—what it represented and who it was for—remained largely the same.

I remember being on vacation in Jamaica in July 2018 and finding that even there, my mind was on my new job as director of CTE. I was researching other districts, brainstorming with my sister about what could be done differently. The question I kept returning to was simple: How can we change this? Because I knew that continuing to do what had always been done would only produce the same results.

To understand how we arrived at this point, we have to examine the systems that shaped it. For decades, the dominant narrative in education centered on college as the primary definition of success. Course offerings, counseling conversations, accountability measures, parental expectations, and public recognition all aligned around that goal. College acceptance became the visible marker of achievement. But the issue isn't the promotion of college—it's the imbalance in how CTE has been presented over time.

To understand where the perception problem began, we have to go back further than a scheduling decision or a single moment. We have to go back to a word. Depending on when you graduated from high school, that word lands differently: vocational. For some people, that word conjures the image of auto mechanics and welding—skilled trades that were valuable but understood at the time as a separate track from the college-bound path. For others, it carries a different association entirely—something remedial, something for students who couldn't make it in the traditional academic setting. That perception didn't come from nowhere. It came from a system that positioned vocational education as the alternative to academic education rather than as an equally rigorous pathway to a meaningful future.

And here's the challenge: Career and Technical Education has evolved dramatically since then. We are not your grandparent's vocational program. We are health science and engineering and digital communications and maritime and real estate and cosmetology and veterinary science and business management and entrepreneurship. We are dual credit and industry-based certifications and work-based learning and Level I postsecondary certificates.

But when someone hears CTE and filters it through the lens of what vocational education meant when they were in high school, they aren't seeing what we've built. They're seeing what they remember. And what they remember isn't what we are. That gap between what CTE was and what CTE is—filtered through the lens of personal experience and generational memory—is where the perception problem lives at its deepest level. People don't look at CTE objectively. They look at it from their own perspective. And their perspective was formed long before they ever walked through our doors.

To understand why that memory is so persistent, we have to go back further than a name. We have to go back to the foundation.

Career and Technical Education—or what was then called vocational education—was not accidentally shaped around gender and class. It was deliberately designed that way. The Smith-Hughes National Vocational Education Act of 1917 was the first federal legislation to fund vocational education in the United States. And from the very beginning, it drew lines. Boys were directed toward agriculture, trades, and industry. Girls were directed toward home economics. The pathways weren't just separate. They were codified by law. A boy who showed academic promise was directed toward college preparation. A boy who struggled was directed toward the shop. A girl—regardless of her aptitude or her ambition—was directed toward the kitchen and the sewing room. The system didn't ask what a student was capable of. It decided in advance what they were destined for.

That isn't ancient history. That's the foundation on which Career and Technical Education was built. And foundations don't disappear when you renovate the house. They remain underneath everything—shaping what feels normal, what feels expected, and what feels like it belongs.

The tracking systems that followed deepened the problem. As academic and vocational tracks became more formalized in schools across the country, a pattern emerged that would define the perception of vocational education for generations: The students who were placed in vocational courses were disproportionately the students who were struggling in the traditional academic setting. Not because vocational education was designed for struggling students. But because the system communicated—through scheduling, through counseling conversations, through where resources were directed and where they were not—that the academic track was for students who could succeed and the vocational track was for students who could not.

That message wasn't written in any policy document, but it was received with perfect clarity by every student, every parent, and every counselor who moved through those systems. And it was received so consistently, over so many decades, that it stopped feeling like a message. It started feeling like a fact.

The gendered history of CTE is equally important because it shaped not just who was tracked into certain pathways but who was allowed to lead within them. Trades were a man's world. Not metaphorically but structurally.

The legislation said so. The culture reinforced it. And for decades, the image of a CTE student in a technical program was a young man in a shop class—not a young woman, whose presence in that space might challenge the assumptions the system had already made about who belonged there.

That image has consequences that outlast the policies that created it. Many still associate Career and Technical Education with low-status or dirty jobs.[1] That association didn't appear out of nowhere. It was built deliberately—through legislation, through tracking systems, and through decades of messaging that

1 Catherine Gewertz, "Stigma Hobbles Career and Technical Education," *Education Week*, May 2017, https://www.edweek.org/teaching-learning/stigma-hobbles-career-and-technical-education/2017/05.

communicated exactly who CTE was for and who it wasn't for. The stigma outlived the system that created it.

When a parent hears CTE and pictures a shop class from thirty years ago, they aren't being irrational. They're responding to a picture the system painted—deliberately, consistently, and over generations. When a counselor hesitates before recommending a CTE pathway to a high-achieving student, that hesitation has roots. When a young woman walks into a welding lab and feels like she doesn't belong there, that feeling didn't come from nowhere. It came from a system that spent decades telling her through structure, through culture, and through law that she did not.

This is why the work of changing perception isn't simply a marketing challenge. It's a historical reckoning. We aren't just trying to tell a better story about CTE. We're trying to undo a story that was told—loudly, consistently, and with the full weight of federal legislation behind it—for more than a century.

And we're making progress. The fact that one of our welding teachers today is a woman who came through our own program isn't just a success story. It's a direct challenge to a system that was designed to keep her out. Every high-achieving student who chooses a CTE pathway is pushing back against a tracking system that was never designed with them in mind. Every industry-based certification earned by a student who was told—explicitly or implicitly—that this pathway was not for someone like them is proof that the foundation, however deeply laid, isn't permanent. Perception was built, which means perception can be changed. But only if we're honest about where it came from.

Perception work is not new to Career and Technical Education. The student organizations that live inside CTE have been navigating it for generations. Long before education leaders were having conversations about narrative and positioning, the organizations themselves were already making hard decisions about how they were being seen and what to do about it.

Consider what happened when Future Homemakers of America (FHA), founded in June 1945, made the decision in July 1999 to change its name to Family, Career and Community Leaders of America (FCCLA). The mission hadn't changed. The students hadn't changed. The commitment to family, community, and service hadn't changed. But leadership recognized something important: The name itself was carrying a perception problem. It was limiting who saw themselves in the organization. It was signaling something narrower than what the work actually was. And after fifty-four years, the organization made the decision to change it—not the substance, not the values, not the work. The story.

That's exactly what this book is asking education leaders to do. Not to abandon what CTE is but to examine honestly how it's being received. And to be willing to make deliberate, sometimes uncomfortable changes to how it's presented.

If an organization that had existed for fifty-four years could look at its own name and say "This is getting in the way of our mission," then so can we. The question is whether we're willing to be that honest—and that brave.

One of the most influential systems that contributed to this perception is scheduling. I remember a student who came to me eager and clear-eyed about her future. She had identified a CTE course that aligned directly with her interests and her goals. But when we looked at her schedule, that course conflicted with an advanced academic course her counselor had strongly recommended. Because the academic course was scheduled at a specific time—what we call a "singleton"—she wasn't being asked to choose between two courses. She was being asked to choose between two versions of what the school believed her future should look like.

Now, I understand that students can't take every course that interests them, and there will always be difficult scheduling decisions. But if the academic course wasn't a graduation requirement and the CTE course aligns with the student's career goals or passion—the choice should be clearer. That isn't a scheduling conflict. That's a perception problem embedded in the structure of the school day.

> ***Perception is not created by one decision. It's built through a thousand small ones.***

I saw this again when working with a high school principal. As we discussed scheduling and the CTE master schedule, she made a statement that stayed with me: Her campus was a "college-bound campus." She said it with conviction, as a point of pride. But underneath that statement were assumptions—that college and CTE were separate, that one held more value than the other, and that her campus had chosen a side. Those beliefs shaped every scheduling decision, every counseling conversation, and every signal sent to students about which paths were worth pursuing. What I wanted her to understand—what I want every leader to understand—is that it's not us versus them. It's not college versus CTE. Students can have both. They do have both. And our systems should reflect that truth.

Parents also play a significant role. Our CTE Center counselor, Priscilla Petetan, has worked with students who were genuinely excited about enrolling in programs at the CTE Center. They would sign up, express interest, and begin to see themselves in those pathways. Then, before the school year began, their names would be removed. When I followed up, the reason was often the same: Their parents didn't want them to attend. Not because the programs lacked value but because the parents didn't fully understand what those programs represented. And without that understanding, they defaulted to what felt safer and more familiar. This happened not once or twice but consistently, year after year. That pattern told me something important: We weren't losing students. We were losing parents. And if we didn't address the parent, we couldn't reach the student.

Messaging plays a critical role in reinforcing this perception. The words we use matter, but so does what we choose to celebrate. I remember sitting at the 2023 district convocation, the kickoff to the school year where bands and drill teams pump teachers up and campuses arrive dressed in school colors with costumes, props, and chants to energize their teams for the year ahead. That year the theme was "Future Ready." I watched as teachers were recognized for student achievement on the State of Texas Assessments of Academic Readiness—known as STAAR—and my team and I were taken aback. I remember asking a question that wouldn't leave me: If we celebrated teachers for high STAAR scores, why weren't we recognizing our IBC teachers in the same way? If we wanted our students to be "Future Ready"—as the convocation t-shirts said—then why weren't we recognizing CTE teachers the same way we recognized core teachers? It was a missed opportunity. The district was working to make future readiness the responsibility of every level—elementary, middle school, and high school—not just the high school years. But a district that promotes future readiness across every grade level and doesn't celebrate the teachers producing industry-based certifications is sending a message, whether it intends to or not.

I didn't have to look far for proof that the perception problem lived inside our own system. Early one morning, one of my coordinators sent me a message: a campus had decided to postpone an IBC bootcamp until after STAAR. The reasoning was clear—STAAR came first. The bootcamp could wait.

But here's what that decision actually said: that an industry-based certification preparing students for a credential with the same accountability weight as STAAR was less urgent than STAAR itself. Another campus had already figured out that you don't have to choose. They were running two IBC bootcamps—during the same STAAR testing window—because they understood that both mattered equally. My coordinator put it simply: "Once again showing that there's no understanding that IBC is the same weight as STAAR."

She was right. The students on that campus were paying the price for a decision that was made without ever considering what they were losing. That wasn't a scheduling decision. That was a perception decision.

I saw this same pattern play out in a way that was impossible to ignore. After comparing the CTE programs at both of our high schools, I discovered that one campus had significantly fewer CTE courses than the other. I was informed that the principal had repurposed CTE positions and converted them into core course sections. It wasn't done out of malice. It was done out of priority. When a leader has to make a choice between staffing a CTE course and staffing an English or math class, they will almost always choose the core subject—because that's where accountability lives, that's where test scores are measured, and that's where pressure from above is felt most acutely. Nobody had to say CTE matters less. The schedule said it for them. And every student on that campus received the message without a single word being spoken.

CTE generates funding. The Carl D. Perkins Career and Technical Education Act—known as Perkins V—is the primary federal legislation that provides funding to states and districts to support CTE programs. Federal Perkins funds, state allocations, and enrollment-based revenue all flow through Career and Technical Education. And that funding matters. It's how we keep our teachers. It's how we purchase equipment, build labs, and sustain the programs that change students' lives. Funding is not the enemy. Funding is the foundation.

But funding should never become the driver of decisions that should be driven by student outcomes. When districts offer CTE courses primarily to capture funding rather than to build genuine programs of study—when seats are filled without sequencing, when teachers are placed without support, when programs exist on paper but not in practice—the funding arrives, but the students pay the price. A program that exists for the budget line and not for the student isn't a CTE program. It's a revenue strategy wearing one. And students know the difference. They can feel when a program has been built for them and when it has been built around them as an afterthought.

Be intentional about how you set your programs up. Because the question isn't just how much funding CTE generates but what that funding is actually building. Funding should follow program quality, not the other way around.

Relevance and recognition cannot start with the director of CTE. They have to start with the superintendent, the cabinet, the principals, and the school board. When the people with the most power treat CTE as a priority, everyone else follows. If the system does not perceive CTE to be as important as English, math, science, and social studies, then a director advocating alone will only go so far.

After four years in the role, it was clear: We still had a perception problem. One of the steps I took was requesting that the IBC testing dates be embedded into the district assessment schedule—not as addendums at the bottom, not as afterthoughts, but as equals. Because when IBC testing sits alongside STAAR testing in the same document, it sends a message to every principal, every counselor, and every teacher about what this district values. I also advocated for IBC testing to be listed on the district instructional calendar the same way STAAR test dates are listed. There are, of course, other assessments districts administer—AP exams, TELPAS, etc. But when none of them are mentioned with the same level of urgency and visibility as STAAR testing, it creates a perception that STAAR is the only test that truly matters. That's how systems communicate priority: not through speeches but through structure.

I'm not blaming anyone. I'm holding up a mirror. And mirrors sometimes show us things we would rather not see. That isn't offensive. That's leadership.

I learned something important through eight years of advocating for Career and Technical Education inside a system that didn't always move at the speed I needed it to: Campus leadership matters more than most people realize. A principal who doesn't believe in CTE will not champion it, will not protect it in the schedule, and will not celebrate it the way it deserves to be celebrated. I encountered a principal who resisted change. Who was set in their ways. Who—whether intentionally or not—blocked the path forward simply by standing still. I couldn't move them. I couldn't convince them. And I couldn't wait for them.

So, I did something else entirely. I moved with the change I could create. I found the spaces where the work could grow, and I grew it there. I built what could be built while others were deciding whether to believe in it. And by the time the resistance caught up to the reality I had already created, the results were already speaking for themselves. That's not giving up on the system. That's understanding how systems actually change. Not all at once. Not by force. But steadily, consistently, and by the people who refuse to stop moving even when the path is blocked. If you're waiting for everyone to get on board before you begin, you'll be waiting forever. Move with the change you can create. The results will do the convincing.

The structural argument for CTE's place alongside college preparation isn't just philosophical; it's built into the state accountability system itself. In Texas, the College, Career, and Military Readiness framework—CCMR—recognizes three equally valid pathways to graduation readiness. College ready. Career ready. Military ready. A student who earns an industry-based certification or a Level I certificate has earned their CCMR point—the same way a student who scores a 3, 4, or 5 on an Advanced Placement (AP) exam has earned theirs. In other words, the system already values CTE achievement.

The problem is that nobody is saying it out loud. When counselors present college prep with urgency and CTE with hesitation, the message students receive isn't what the accountability system actually says. The structure says CTE counts, but the culture isn't reflecting it. That gap is where perception lives.

Do I give up, or do I keep speaking up for what I believe can help move the perception needle? I choose to keep speaking up. Because, as a product of this district, I know that CTE is valued here. I have seen it. I have lived it. But knowing something is valued and showing that it's valued are two different things. And until our systems, our schedules, our celebrations, and our structures reflect what we say we believe, the perception gap will remain. That is not a reason to stop. It's a reason to speak louder.

Robert Greene writes in *The 48 Laws of Power*—a national bestseller on power, strategy, and human behavior—that we must preach the need for change but never reform too much at once. That principle applies here. The perception problem was not created in a day, and it will not be solved in one either. Change that lasts requires patience, consistency, and a clear understanding of the patterns you're trying to shift before you try to shift them. Leaders who rush to fix everything at once often create resistance that sets the work back further than it was before. The goal isn't a dramatic overhaul. It's a deliberate, sustained shift that moves the system in the right direction without triggering the fear that causes people to dig in and hold on to what's familiar.

Over time, I began to understand that perception is built through patterns. It's shaped by what's emphasized, what's prioritized, and what's consistently reinforced. The challenge is that these patterns often go unnoticed. Educators and leaders believe they're supporting all pathways equally, while the lived experience of students tells a different story. Once we recognize how perception has been created, we're in a position to change it.

CHAPTER 3

THE HIDDEN MESSAGES SCHOOLS SEND STUDENTS

What students actually experience vs. what we think we're saying

Schools communicate far more than what is written in lesson plans or stated in mission statements. Every day, through routines, structures, conversations, and experiences, students are receiving messages about what matters, what's valued, and what success looks like. These messages aren't always spoken directly. In fact, the most powerful ones rarely are. They're embedded in what students see, what they hear, and what they experience consistently over time.

There's a significant gap between what we believe we're saying and what students are actually hearing. That gap is where perception is formed—and where it takes root.

One of the most powerful ways schools send hidden messages is through how success is defined and celebrated. Academic achievements are highly visible. Honor roll lists are posted. Test scores are announced. College acceptance letters are shared publicly with ceremony and pride. These celebrations are meaningful and deserve recognition. However, when CTE achievements aren't elevated in the same way, it creates an imbalance that students notice and interpret. Students who earn industry-based certifications—credentials that could immediately impact their future—often received little to no public recognition. Both groups accomplish something significant, but only one group is fully seen. Students notice that.

> ***Students don't hear what we intend to say. They hear what the system consistently shows them.***

This is precisely why we created the CTE Choice Awards. When a member of the CTE team suggested we use the administration building for the first year and then move to a larger venue later, I said clearly, "No, they will not come." If we wanted families to attend, if we wanted students to feel celebrated, we had to create something worthy of those accomplishments from the very beginning. So, we went big. We pulled out the red carpet—literally. We hosted a red-carpet hour where we interviewed students, parents, and guests. We brought in a keynote speaker who was a graduate of one of the Beaumont ISD high schools so students could hear from someone who once walked the same halls they did. We had a DJ, vendors, photo booths, professional decor, a photographer, and a semi-formal dress code. My team wore black and bling. We selected the Beaumont Event Centre—a venue many local schools use for prom, including the high school where I once served as principal—so I knew exactly the kind of experience I could offer those students.

For many of them, it was the first time they'd been honored in that way before their families and community. I'm proud to say that the first year we were filled to capacity. The next few years, we had to move the CTE Choice Awards to the Beaumont Civic Center to accommodate more people. The feedback was fulfilling in ways I didn't anticipate. Teachers finally felt appreciated. Students were excited to receive their red-carpet awards and their IBC cords—cords they could wear at graduation. While the event is primarily for juniors and seniors, the excitement those students brought back to campus became our best marketing to underclassmen who wanted to be in that room one day.

The awards we created were designed to recognize every dimension of CTE excellence. The Best Teacher Performance award goes to the teacher whose students achieved a one hundred percent pass rate on their industry-based certification exams. The Stand Out Performer award recognizes the teacher whose students earned the highest number of industry-based certifications. The Best Student Performance award honors the student who has earned the most industry-based certifications. The Blockbuster Student Performance award recognizes outstanding achievement within a CTSO (Career and Technical Student Organization) from state and national competitions. The Hidden Star award honors a staff member who performs above and beyond in a selfless manner to prepare students for success. The Breakthrough Star recognizes a first-year CTE teacher who's had a breakthrough year. The Rising Star goes to a first-year middle school CTE teacher who has displayed exceptional promise. The Walk of Fame recognizes a teacher who has stepped up with vision and initiative to bring a new course to life. The Best Supporting Role is presented to an individual whose support has been vital to the success of the event—always ready to lend a hand, always saying yes, and consistently showing up with a spirit of service.

We also recognize our Student Icon and Teacher Icon award recipients—individuals whose impact on Career and Technical Education goes beyond a single accomplishment or a single year. These are the students and teachers who have become the face of CTE when it's fully believed in and fully lived. Every year we also honor our Business and Industry Partner of the Year—the company or individual whose commitment to our students and our programs has gone above and beyond what partnership requires. Because without industry partners who show up, invest, and advocate, the pipeline from classroom to career doesn't exist. These awards remind every person in that room that CTE isn't a school department. It's a community effort.

And, finally, the Fan Favorite Award represents the students' voice—nearly 500 students casting their votes for the CTE teacher who made the greatest impact on their lives.

Each year at the CTE Choice Awards, we also take time to highlight and recognize individuals and departments from across the district who were instrumental in helping us carry out the mission of CTE at the highest level. Not departments doing the minimum. Not colleagues checking a box. We're talking about the people who went the extra mile, who showed up for CTE students, who advocated in rooms where CTE wasn't always the priority, and who used their platform and their position to elevate what we're building together.

The Best Supporting Role award is presented each year to an individual or department outside of CTE whose contribution to our students goes above and beyond what their job requires. Over the years, that recognition has gone to our Early Childhood, Health Services, Human Resources, and Transportation departments—teams that had every reason to stay in their own lane and chose instead to show up for ours. Early Childhood helped us connect practicum students with local daycares for their Child Development Associate credential, building real work-based learning experiences for students pursuing careers in early childhood education and giving them access to the hours and the environments they needed to earn that certification before they ever graduated. Health Services has certified our eleventh-grade health science students in Basic Life Support and CPR, ensuring they're ready to begin their hospital rotations before they graduate. Human Resources partnered with us to ensure our students were fingerprinted for their Law and Teaching and Training pathways (for those pursuing their Educational Aide Certification), making it possible for students to access real professional environments before graduation. And Transportation made sure our practicum students who had hospital rotations could get there. Because access means nothing if a student cannot physically reach the program.

The Best Supporting Cast award recognizes a group of individuals who operate behind the scenes but hold the CTE department together—our CTE administrative support staff whose work makes everything else possible. Because changing perception is never the work of one department alone. And when the people around you go beyond what is required to support what you believe in—that deserves to be seen, named, and celebrated in front of everyone.

The IBC Cording Ceremony is one of the most powerful moments of the CTE Choice Awards, and it's led by my coordinator of CTE, Alicia Green, who has championed industry-based certifications since long before the rest of the system caught up. Each year, she stands before that room and makes the case that an IBC is not a participation award or a classroom grade. It's a credential recognized by business and industry at the local, state, and national level—proof that a student has demonstrated mastery in a specific skill set that employers value and industries recognize. In one recent year alone, 26 CTE teachers certified 320 seniors with over 400 industry-based certifications. Every single one of those seniors passed. Each one received a green cord—worn first on the CTE Choice Awards stage and then again at graduation. When students cross that graduation stage wearing that cord, the community sees something it may not have seen before: a graduate who isn't just diploma ready. They're career ready. And there's a credential around their neck to prove it.

I call the IBC the "grown folk test." Because that's exactly what it is. The same assessment that a working adult takes to enter an industry—to get licensed, to get certified, to get hired—is the same test that our seventeen- and eighteen-year-old students are sitting down and passing. Let that sink in. These aren't simplified versions designed for high schoolers. They're the real thing. And our students are passing them. That isn't a small accomplishment. That's a statement about who our students are and what they're capable of when the system around them communicates that they're capable of it.

Due to social media and news media coverage, other districts called me to learn more about the CTE Choice Awards. That evening wasn't just about recognition. It was about changing what people saw. And when people see something differently, they begin to believe something differently.

Another powerful source of hidden messages is exposure—or the lack of it. For too long, career day was treated as a check-the-box event. A fire truck pulled up to the cafeteria, students rotated through a few stations, and then the day ended. No follow-up. No connection. No one ever talked about firefighting again, or any other career for that matter. That kind of exposure doesn't shape perception. It creates a token gesture that students recognize as exactly that.

Students need consistent, meaningful experiences that allow them to see, touch, and interact with different pathways. For several years, my team hosted the College, Career, and Military Readiness (CCMR) Fair on a Saturday during CTE Month in February for our entire community. But we decided that event didn't provide enough touch points, so our schools were charged to host a CCMR fair on their respective campuses. For the CTE department, we shifted our approach through our K–8 Career Readiness initiative, bringing CTE directly to students in what we called the CTE Road Show. My K–8 Career Readiness specialist, Shamine Cormier, brought equipment, simulations, demonstrations, and experiences directly to elementary and middle school campuses so that students could see it, touch it, and feel what it meant to be part of these fields. When students can see it, they can begin to believe it.

The CTE Road Show was an immediate hit, and we had to figure out how to scale it. We created the Future Ready Lab, setting up those same equipment, simulations, demonstrations, and experiences at the CTE Center. Elementary and middle schools were now able to transport their students to us, ensuring that our K–8 students were exposed to the pathways we offer in our district and the job opportunities available in our community.

In addition to recognition, hidden messages are also communicated through conversations in ways that are almost invisible. I remember observing a counseling session where a student expressed interest in a CTE pathway. The counselor was supportive—genuinely so—but the support came wrapped in hesitation. The conversation shifted almost immediately toward "keeping options open" and ensuring the student had enough traditional academic courses on her schedule. It was well-meaning, but the student didn't hear well-meaning. She heard uncertainty. She heard that the path she was excited about might not be enough on its own. And that doubt, planted in a single conversation by someone she trusted, is exactly how perception takes root.

There's a term that gets used in education that most people never say out loud in a meeting but everyone understands in practice: sacred cows. Some classes are considered sacred cows, meaning we don't touch them. We don't question their scheduling priority. We don't examine whether they're serving students as well as we believe. We simply protect them. And in a system where certain classes are untouchable, every other class—including CTE—communicates its own message by contrast. If some programs are sacred, then others are expendable. Students absorb that hierarchy without anyone ever saying it directly. That's exactly how perception works. It doesn't need a memo. It just needs a system that keeps reinforcing the same unspoken message year after year.

I want to share something that happened while I was doing research for this very book. I was at one of our high schools looking for old yearbooks. I asked a staff member where I could find them. She directed me to the journalism classroom. I told her I didn't want to disrupt the class. And she said—without hesitation, without any awareness of what she was communicating—"Oh, it's okay. She teaches journalism; it's not a core class. This is what they do. This is where they sell the yearbooks."

Journalism. The class that teaches students to write, report, interview, research, produce, and communicate. The class that designed, photographed, and produced the very yearbook I was standing there trying to buy. The class that in many districts feeds directly into broadcast, media, communications, and digital marketing pathways. Not a core class. Just the place where they sell the yearbooks.

I told her to please not say that.

I want to be clear: Her comment was harmless. She meant nothing by it. She was being helpful and kind. But that's exactly the point. If someone had overheard that exchange and internalized it, the message they would have received is this: It's not okay to interrupt a core class, but it's perfectly fine to walk into a journalism class unannounced because what happens in there is less important. That's not what she meant. But that's what perception does. It takes a casual, well-intentioned comment and turns it into a signal—one that students, teachers, and administrators absorb without anyone ever meaning to send it.

That statement—said casually, said without malice, said as a courtesy—is the entire argument of this book in a single sentence. The perception problem isn't something that happened in the past and left a residue we're still cleaning up. It's happening right now. In 2026. In the hallways of our own schools. By people who genuinely mean well and have no idea what they're communicating.

That's why this work is never finished. And that's why it matters.

Industry-based certification testing is the same assessment that working adults take to enter their fields. The same test that our seventeen- and eighteen-year-old students sit down and pass. When STAAR testing happens, it's all hands on deck. Principals show up. District monitors are assigned to campuses. They walk the halls. They check in. They communicate by their presence that this moment matters. When IBC testing happens, it's only the CTE team on deck. It feels like we aren't supported. Nobody said CTE certification day is less important than other state testing days. Nobody had to. The absence communicates it. That isn't a scheduling oversight. That's a perception problem.

I want to be clear: I don't believe this comes from a lack of care. Most principals and district leaders genuinely want their students to succeed in every pathway. But good intentions don't change the message that's received. And until IBC testing is treated with the same urgency and visibility as other state testing, the message CTE students and CTE teachers receive will remain the same. That's the work ahead.

I also saw the contrast through my daughter's CTE experience. She was a dual-credit, fine arts student and leader like her brother—a three-year drill team member, junior lieutenant, and captain her senior year. It was not us versus them, fine arts versus CTE. Both lived in her simultaneously. She took business and real estate classes, earned her Entrepreneurship and Small Business (ESB) certification her senior year, and is working on finishing her real estate courses to become a REALTOR® through the National Association of Realtors®. My husband owns a construction company, and I am a REALTOR®. With the skills my daughter learned in her real estate classes, she was able to assist me in showing a home during an open house—and she was really good! She was a natural, and because of that hands-on experience, she found a deeper love for real estate. And I say this with every bit of pride a mother can hold: She is better than me at this. She applied what she learned through her ESB certification and is now a business owner. She's a social media influencer with a management company, and she started building her brand during her senior year. She's now a sophomore business and marketing major at the University of Houston, securing partnerships and stepping into opportunities that align with her skills. Today, she has brand deals with Ulta Beauty at Target, Capital One, and Kate Spade, just to name a few, and she had a casting opportunity on a Netflix shopping show. That's what happens when students receive both access to CTE and belief in CTE. They don't just learn—they *become* CTE.

The physical environment also contributes to perception in ways leaders often overlook. What's displayed on walls, what's highlighted in newsletters, what's promoted during events, what's shown on the jumbotron at football games—all of this shapes the student experience. When academic achievements dominate those spaces, it reinforces a hierarchy of value that students absorb without anyone having to say a single word. Closing that gap requires intentional action. This is why our CTE teachers serve as our CTE social media liaisons for our CTE social media pages and YouTube channel—so we can tell our own stories. It requires aligning what students see, hear, and feel with a consistent message that all pathways are valued and all achievement is worth celebrating.

PART

02

UNDERSTANDING THE INFLUENCE

C — Clarify the Value of CTE | E — Elevate Awareness of Influences

CHAPTER 4

WHY STUDENTS CHOOSE WHAT THEY CHOOSE

Perception drives decisions more than data

Dr. Allen and I often have the same question: How do we make students want what we know they need? It's one of the most honest questions in education, and it doesn't have a simple answer. Understanding why students make the choices they do requires looking beyond the options themselves. It requires examining what those options represent to the students making them. At the heart of every educational decision isn't logic or data. It's perception. Students aren't simply selecting programs based on outcomes or earning potential. They're choosing based on what they believe those programs say about them—about their intelligence, their future, and their place in the world.

I want to make this concrete because abstract arguments rarely change minds. Consider my husband Michael. He worked in the elevator industry, which is generally considered the highest-paying trade in the United States. He had a six-figure salary with a high school diploma and a certificate from the national elevator industry trade school with no student debt. During a junior parent meeting when I was a high school principal, I compared his salary to mine. He out-earned me. A high school diploma and a trade certificate versus a doctorate, two master's degrees, a bachelor's, an associate of science degree, and four certifications. The room got very quiet.

Students who may have been quietly dismissing the trades reconsidered. Parents who may have been directing their children away from technical careers paused. Why? Because for the first time, they were seeing a real person, a real number, and a real comparison. Not a brochure. Not a statistic. A story. That's the difference between information and belief. Information exists everywhere. Belief requires experience. And in that moment, the experience was undeniable: A man with a high school diploma and a trade certification was earning nearly double what a woman with a doctorate was earning. Nobody had a rebuttal. Nobody needed one. The numbers told the story.

Students don't choose what they don't believe in. Our job is to build belief before they reach the decision.

But here's what makes the challenge even more layered: Many students don't choose against CTE because they've weighed the options and decided it's not for them. They choose against it because they don't fully understand what it is. Ask a room full of high school students what an Advanced Placement (AP) exam is, and every hand goes up. Ask them what an IBC is, and you'll often be met with silence or confusion. They know AP because the system has communicated its value clearly, consistently, and loudly. They've been told what it means, what it leads to, and why it matters. The IBC—the industry-based certification that can qualify a student for immediate employment, industry recognition, and in many cases a wage premium—has not always received that same treatment.

Instead, CTE has often been communicated as something else entirely. An elective. An easy A. A GPA booster for students who need a break from rigorous coursework. I've heard those descriptions from students, from parents, and—if I'm being honest—from educators who should have known better.

I received a phone call from a parent complaining about the amount of homework his daughter was receiving in her culinary arts class. He was frustrated. The workload felt excessive to him—more than he expected from a CTE course. And I remember thinking, *This parent called to complain that his daughter had too much work in a CTE class. Not too little. Not that the class wasn't challenging enough. Too much.*

That phone call told me something important. This parent had enrolled his daughter in culinary arts expecting it to be easy. He had received the same message that so many families had received—that CTE was the lighter option, the breather in an otherwise demanding schedule. He wasn't calling because he didn't value education. He was calling because the experience didn't match the expectation he'd been given. And that expectation had been shaped long before his daughter ever set foot in that classroom.

That's the cost of the perception problem. When CTE is communicated as an elective, a break, an easy A, and then a student walks in and discovers it's actually rigorous, demanding, and real, the response isn't always gratitude. Sometimes it's a phone call. Not because the teacher did anything wrong. But because the narrative that preceded the class set the wrong expectation entirely.

I received an email in the summer of 2022 from a student who was in the top 4 percent of her class and planning to attend Texas A&M in the fall. She was enrolled in a CTE work program and was concerned about how it would affect her class ranking. She asked me to make the course weighted again because she was worried it would hurt her GPA and her standing. She wasn't writing because she didn't believe in the program. She was writing because the system had communicated to her—and to her parents—that CTE courses weren't weighted the same way as other rigorous coursework. That perception didn't come from nowhere. It came from the way we'd structured and communicated the value of CTE pathways for years.

My response was simple: All weighted CTE courses are technical, dual-credit courses only. But the email itself told me something far more important than any policy question. Here was a high-achieving student, headed to one of the best business schools in Texas, enrolled in a CTE work program because she saw the value in real-world experience—and she was worried about what it would cost her. That isn't a student problem. That's a perception problem. And it's exactly the kind of signal that leaders have to be paying attention to.

When students believe a course is there to fill a schedule and boost a grade, they don't choose it because they believe in its value. They choose it in spite of what they believe about it. And that distinction matters because a student who enrolls out of convenience isn't the same as a student who enrolls out of conviction. Conviction leads to completion. Conviction leads to certification. Conviction leads to careers.

The beliefs that shape student choices don't originate only in the classroom. They begin in living rooms, at dinner tables, and in the casual conversations adults have when they think no one is paying attention. One of my colleagues was at a volleyball tournament and struck up a conversation with another parent who happened to be an administrator at a different school district. When the conversation turned to work, that administrator said plainly, "We don't care about CTE." Not as a confession. Not with any apparent awareness of what that statement revealed. Just as a statement of fact, the way you might describe your district's focus or priorities. That administrator went home that night and returned to a school where students, counselors, and teachers would receive—through a thousand small signals—that same message. And those students would make decisions accordingly.

This is how perception travels. It doesn't need a policy memo or a formal directive. It moves through the attitudes of the adults in the room. It moves through what's said casually at a volleyball tournament, at a staff meeting, in the counseling office, or at a kitchen table. Students aren't just responding to what the system offers. They're responding to what the adults around them believe the system is worth.

> ***Students aren't just responding to what the system offers. They're responding to what the adults around them believe the system is worth.***

I know this firsthand because I was once one of those adults. Before I became a director of CTE, I was a high school counselor, and my job was to make sure my students had enough credits to graduate. As long as they graduated, I fulfilled my role. But did I do my best to ensure they were enrolled in the right CTE courses—courses aligned with their interests, their strengths, and their future? Did I schedule them based on their passions or based on what the graduation requirements demanded? That's the harder question. And if I's being honest, the answer isn't always what I wish it were.

I'll be honest with you about my time as a high school principal in a way I think this work requires: I was guilty of the stigma. My primary focus was on English, math, science, and social studies. That's where accountability lived at the time. That's where test scores were measured, where campus ratings were determined, how I was evaluated by the superintendent, and where attention and resources naturally flowed. CTE was present on my campus, but it wasn't always centered. I didn't dismiss it. I didn't discourage it. I supported it, and I assigned an assistant principal who was CTE-certified as the CTE administrator, a person who had also worked under the stigma of being seen as "just an elective teacher." From the lens of a principal, your focus goes where accountability goes. But because I was a former CTE teacher, because I know what it feels like for CTE to be in the background, they knew I was on their side. I made sure they were respected, heard, and able to get the supplies they needed without feeling less than. But because accountability didn't sit with CTE, the system forced me to shift my priority to where the greatest level of urgency lay.

What changed my understanding was becoming responsible for CTE. When I stepped into the director of CTE role and began to see CTE from the inside—its rigor, its outcomes, its industry connections, its impact on students' lives—I understood for the first time the cost of my earlier neutrality. I had been leading a campus where students were making decisions about their futures, and I hadn't given Career and Technical Education the visibility, the advocacy, or the equal footing it deserved. I share this not as a confession that ends with guilt but as a recognition that ends with responsibility. Because if a principal who genuinely cared about students could still contribute to the perception problem without realizing it, then this issue is not about intent. It's about awareness. And awareness is something we can choose to build.

In Texas, CTE is now 40 percent of accountability, just like core academic subjects. That's not a footnote. That's a statement about the value the state of Texas has assigned to Career and Technical Education. But policy alone doesn't change perception. Leaders do. And the first step is being honest enough to examine what we've believed, what we've communicated, and what we've allowed students to absorb—even when we thought we were neutral. If you don't champion it, someone else's silence will define it. And in the absence of a champion, perception fills the void.

Students choose what they believe in. They believe what they're shown consistently, what they hear affirmed by the adults they trust, and what they see reflected in the systems around them. If we want to change what students choose, we have to change what they believe. And if we want to change what they believe, we have to start with ourselves—with the messages we're sending, the stories we're telling, and the value we're visibly, consistently, unapologetically assigning to Career and Technical Education.

The culture is already shifting. In 2025, only 35 percent of Americans said a four-year college degree was very important[2]—a significant drop from previous generations. Students and families are beginning to question whether the traditional pathway is the only pathway worth choosing. The perception is changing outside the school. The question is whether it's changing inside.

Danny Meyer, the restaurateur behind some of New York's most celebrated dining experiences, built his career on a principle he calls "enlightened hospitality."[3] His argument is simple but profound: People don't choose a restaurant based on the food alone. They choose based on how the experience makes them feel. A meal can be technically perfect and still lose a customer forever if the experience surrounding it communicates that they don't matter. And a meal can be imperfect in every measurable way and still earn a loyal guest for life if the person leaves feeling seen, welcomed, and valued.

That isn't a restaurant principle. That's a perception principle. And it applies directly to Career and Technical Education.

Students don't choose CTE based on programs alone. They choose based on how the pathway makes them feel about themselves. A program can be technically rigorous, industry-aligned, and credential-producing yet still go unchosen if the experience surrounding it communicates that selecting it means something less about who they are. And a pathway can be newer, smaller, and still developing yet still fill seats if every student who encounters it walks away feeling like they belong there and that choosing it says something good about their future.

---

2 Gallup, "Perceived Importance of College Hits New Low," September 11, 2025, https://news.gallup.com/poll/695003/perceived-importance-college-hits-new-low.aspx.

3 Danny Meyer, *Setting the Table: The Transforming Power of Hospitality in Business* (HarperCollins, 2006).

The food is the program. The experience is the perception. And in education, just like in hospitality, the experience is what determines whether people come back.

No matter how many times I share that we tied the state of Texas in IBCs and surpassed them with Level 1 certificates, that CTE is 40 percent of accountability, that the CTE Center is designed for hands-on learning in industry-standard labs, the data alone doesn't move students. Perception does.

Students don't read program-of-study documents. They respond to what they see, hear, and feel. They choose the class that looks engaging. They choose the teacher who makes it come alive. They choose the pathway someone explained to them clearly. They choose the program that feels like it leads somewhere real. Which means the work at your table is exactly this: not just offering programs but strengthening the conditions that make students choose them. We don't stop at offering programs. We lead them well enough that students want them.

I know this because I watched it happen with my own daughter. When she was in eighth grade, I sat with her and her counselor to select her pathway and program of study. Some of the pathways she was most interested in led to the CTE Center, which would require her to ride the bus from her home campus to the CTE Center every day during her junior and senior year. I explained how it worked, what the programs offered, and what it could lead to. She listened carefully. And then she said, "Oh no, that's too much."

I asked why. She said, "Mom, that's too much movement. Having to ride the bus back and forth to two different campuses is not something I want to do." And then she said the thing that stopped me cold: "Plus, my friends are not going to do that either."

And there it was, the true revelation: Not the logistics. Not the schedule. Not the bus. It was the friends. Students don't just choose programs. They choose identities. They choose communities. They choose what the people they care about will think of them. And until CTE is the place where everyone wants to be, like an AP class, until it carries the kind of social currency that makes a student say "My friends are going to do that" instead of "My friends are not," we haven't finished the work of changing perception.

CHAPTER 5

THE PARENT INFLUENCE NOBODY TALKS ABOUT

Security, fear, and generational beliefs

My mother, Wilma Ree Joseph Powell, was not just a supporter. She was a trailblazer long before I understood what that word meant. Her hard work and persistence paid off when she received a scholarship to attend Blessed Sacrament School in 1956. She was an honor student and graduated in 1960. While there, she was a sodality officer and class officer, a member of the glee club, captain of the drill squad, and a member of the shield staff and yearbook staff. After graduation, she continued her education at Chenier Business College. Her tenaciousness and strong will to succeed carried her further than most people would have dared to go—she became the first African American woman to be employed by the B.F. Goodrich synthetic rubber plant in Port Neches, Texas in 1962. She walked through a door that had never been opened for someone who looked like her and retired after nearly forty years of service. And she did it with the same quiet strength and determination that she poured into every one of her children. When I think about what it means to change perception—to walk into a room where you weren't expected and perform at a level that can't be ignored—I think about her first. She showed me what that looked like long before I had the language to describe it.

My father, Donaldson Leo Powell, graduated from Hebert High School in 1957, the school whose motto—"Whatever Hebert does, it must be the best"—was woven into the fabric of everything he did. During his high school years, he played basketball and ran track. After graduation, he continued his education at Texas College and Prairie View A&M University. He was employed by Millennium Chemicals, and after nearly thirty years of service, he retired in 1996. During his employment, he also served as union vice president and on numerous boards for various charitable organizations, including United Way. He coached and mentored many young men through the Spindletop Football Little League, and to this day, he is still known by many simply as "Coach." That title was not given to him by an organization. It was earned through decades of showing up for young people who needed someone in their corner.

Entrepreneurship was instilled in my dad by his grandparents at an early age. After his retirement, he followed his long-time dream and opened Honey Charter Service—naming the business after his Aunt Josephine, who everyone called "Honey." She was the inspiration behind the name. He loved providing bus transportation services to the community and surrounding areas. Through that business, he developed friendships with clients from churches, schools, and civic organizations across the region. He built something after retirement because that's who he was—someone who never stopped creating, never stopped serving, and never stopped believing that the work in front of him was worth doing well.

Entrepreneurship is in my DNA. My great-grandparents owned a neighborhood corner store—the kind of business that was the heartbeat of the community it served. My father owned rental properties. And from the time I was young, one of my jobs was to ride with him to collect the rent. I wasn't just along for the ride. I had a role, a responsibility. A real task that required me to show up prepared and professional. I didn't know it at the time, but I was learning business. I was learning ownership. I was learning what it meant to build something and protect it. I was a lover of Career and Technical Education long before I ever knew what CTE was. The hands-on, real-world work that CTE is designed to produce—I was already living it. My family had been living it for generations. And when I eventually stood in front of a classroom as a CTE teacher and then behind a director's desk leading a department built around preparing students for exactly that kind of real-world experience, I understood in a deeply personal way why this work matters. It was never foreign to me. It was always home.

When I think about where my drive came from—the persistence, the community investment, the belief that you keep going even when the road is hard—I think about both of my parents. A mother who walked through doors that weren't built for her. A father who coached young men and then built a business and named it after the woman who inspired him. These were my first examples of what it looks like to lead with purpose. Everything I've done in education is built on the foundation they laid.

Parents are one of the most powerful—and often least understood—influences on the decisions students make about their future. While schools design programs, counselors guide course selections, and teachers encourage exploration, parents are often the final voice in whether a student pursues a particular pathway. Their influence isn't always visible within the school system, but it's deeply present in the decisions students ultimately make.

To understand this influence, we have to begin with a simple truth: Most parents aren't trying to limit opportunity. They're trying to protect it. For many families, education is directly connected to security. It represents stability, upward mobility, and the possibility of a better future. Parents want their children to succeed, and they often rely on what they know—or what they've been told—to guide those decisions. For generations, that guidance has centered around a familiar message: Go to college, get a degree, and you'll be successful.

I know this truth personally, and not just as an educator. My father didn't have any boys. He had four girls, and I was born on July 12—his birthday is July 13—so I think I was the closest he got to having a boy. His name is Donaldson Leo, and he named me Donna Lee. He loved sports. Football and track were his favorites. And, without any boys of his own, he did what any loving father would do: He tried to spark an interest in sports in his girls.

He brought my two older sisters to a track meet. When they saw how fast the other girls were— especially Dani from down the street—the tears started falling. Sports weren't their passion. He enrolled me in swim lessons at the L.L. Melton YMCA, where Coach John Clayton, Sr. was my swim coach. I was good. They said I could swim like a fish. I was winning races. But as I got older, my passion for swimming started to drift. I remember a big swim meet where I won, and my dad surprised me with my first dog—a Weimaraner—and I named him Coco. But even that gift couldn't hold my heart in the water. I wanted something different.

When they started offering dance classes at the YMCA, I wanted in. The moment I stepped into that class, I knew. The decision had been made, at least for then. But when I got to middle school, my dad told me that Evelyn Harper was the basketball coach—and she was our cousin. He convinced me to try it out. I want to be clear: Coach Harper being our cousin did me no favors. She was still tough. And she didn't have a problem sitting me on the bench. I can still hear her yelling my name—"Powell!" I played volleyball and basketball in middle school and played clarinet in the band. I could see the excitement in my dad's eyes when he watched his daughter playing sports again. He put a volleyball net in the backyard and installed a basketball goal in the driveway out front. He did what any parent would do—he provided the tools necessary to help his child get better. But I didn't have the drive to practice. It wasn't what I wanted to do.

I remember the neighborhood boys—Kevin, Chris, Byron, Jeffrey, and others—knocking on the door asking to use the goal. They used it far more than I did. Instead of going out there and playing with them to get better, I would watch them. Eventually my dad got tired of watching them use the goal more than I did. It really started to get annoying—as if our front yard was the neighborhood park. I remember the day my dad backed his burgundy El Camino into the yard and pulled the goal down. I can still hear the tires screeching and see the smoke.

But I still tried to make him happy. I played volleyball and basketball my freshman year in high school—until I got in trouble for being somewhere I wasn't supposed to be and my dad made me quit basketball. I must admit I was happy to turn in my basketball uniform because Coach Carolyn Rogers was tough, ran hard practices, and didn't play favorites. And honestly my heart was never really in it anyway. I didn't play sports my sophomore year and then found the courage to try out for the drill team my junior year. I became a member of the West Brook Stars, and my love for dance continued into college. And like my mother before me, I made history. I was one of the founding members of the Lamar University dance team—the LU Sensations—and danced for three years.

That decision—the one I had to make for myself against the current of expectation—changed everything about how I moved through the world. Not because sports were wrong for others but because they weren't right for me. My father wasn't trying to limit me. He was guiding me toward what felt familiar and successful from his perspective. But his perception of what I should do almost replaced my own sense of who I was.

And even though I hadn't followed the athletic path my dad had envisioned for me, both of my parents were at every game I danced at in high school and college. That's the kind of love that doesn't require you to be who they imagined. It just requires showing up. And they always did.

> ***Parents aren't the barrier. They're a critical part of the solution when we bring them into the conversation.***

Fear plays a significant role in this process—not dramatic fear but practical fear. Parents fear their child making the wrong decision. They fear missed opportunities. They fear that choosing a path outside of what's traditionally accepted may lead to instability or regret. Generational beliefs also shape these decisions. Many parents are guiding their children based on their own experiences with education and work. In Southeast Texas, oil and gas is a way of life, and many students follow in their parents' footsteps. Both of my parents worked in the petrochemical industry. When I was growing up, working at the United States Postal Service (USPS) was a family tradition in some households. I knew an entire family that worked for the USPS across two generations.

If parents' understanding of Career and Technical Education is based on what it looked like years ago, they may not recognize how much it has changed. They may not be aware of the certifications available, the partnerships with industry, or the direct pathways to high-demand, high-skill or high-wage careers. Without that awareness, their perception remains tied to the past.

I've had conversations with parents who were genuinely surprised to learn about the earning potential associated with certain technical careers. When I showed them real data—real salaries, real career trajectories, real people like Michael, an elevator mechanic—their perspective shifted. What once felt uncertain began to feel like an opportunity. This is why involving industry partners became such an important part of our work. When advisory council members—people who hire, who understand workforce needs, who see the value of technical skills every day—began speaking to parents, the conversation changed. Their voices carried a level of credibility that connected directly to what parents cared about most: real outcomes for their children.

The high school principal who told me that thirteen- and fourteen-year-olds were too young to select a pathway was expressing a version of this same fear. Her concern was that students at that age were being asked to make consequential decisions before they were ready. I understood that concern. But I also told her this directly: We expect students to make even more significant decisions at eighteen years old—choosing a college, selecting a major, deciding on a career—often with far less structured exposure than a well-designed CTE pathway provides. The difference is not age. The difference is guidance and experience. When students are introduced to pathways early, when they're given opportunities to explore and understand their options, they're better prepared to make informed decisions later. Not more constrained—more confident.

I saw this same pattern play out long before I became a director of CTE. When I was a high school counselor, we were offering the ASVAB Career Exploration Program to our students—a free career assessment administered by the Department of Defense that helps students identify their interests, aptitudes, and potential career pathways. It isn't a military recruitment tool. It's a career exploration tool. But a parent called me and told me directly that his daughter wasn't going into the military and he didn't want her taking the ASVAB. He had heard the word ASVAB and made a decision based on what he believed it meant, without knowing what it actually was. I understood his concern. But I also understood what that moment revealed. A parent who doesn't have the right information will always default to what feels safest, even when what feels safest isn't what is best. That isn't a parenting failure. That's a communication failure. And communication is exactly where the perception problem lives.

Before I ever stood in front of a classroom as a CTE teacher, I sat in one as a CTE student. My mother made me take record keeping, typing, accounting, and shorthand in high school. Not because I chose them. Because she believed every young woman needed those skills. She wasn't wrong by the standards of her time. She was thinking about my future the best way she knew how. I remember the classroom and where I sat. My business teachers were Audrey Holmes and Linda Aplon. Mary Upton taught me accounting, and Linda Holstine was my typing teacher. But nobody presented those courses as a career pathway. Nobody connected them to an industry or a credential or a salary. They were simply what students—particularly young women—were guided toward. And I took them without questioning what they were preparing me for because nobody around me was asking that question either. That's how embedded the perception was. It didn't feel like a system making decisions for me. It felt like just the way things were.

Parents aren't the barrier. When they understand the value of Career and Technical Education, they become advocates. They support their children in exploring pathways they may not have considered. They reinforce the belief that success can take multiple forms. And when students and parents are aligned, decisions become clearer, confidence replaces hesitation, and pathways that were once overlooked become pathways that are chosen with pride.

CHAPTER 6

THE STAFF MINDSET THAT SHAPES EVERYTHING

Counselors, teachers, and leaders as decision-shapers

Within every school system, there's a group of individuals who hold extraordinary influence over the decisions students make: counselors, teachers, and campus leaders. These are the people students listen to, trust, and rely on when navigating their future. Their beliefs, whether spoken or unspoken, shape how students interpret the choices in front of them. Because of this, staff mindset isn't a secondary factor in student decision-making. It's central to it.

Students don't just respond to programs. They respond to people. They respond to how those people present options, how confidently they speak about those options, and what they appear to believe about them. When the adults in a system are aligned in their understanding and belief, students receive a clear and consistent message. When they aren't, students receive mixed signals. Those signals almost always lead to hesitation, and hesitation leads to the safer, more familiar choice.

I saw this with unmistakable clarity when my son told me what his AP teacher had said: The class was "too smart" to go to the CTE Center. That statement wasn't just a comment. It was a belief system about intelligence, about pathways, and about who belongs in certain spaces. She probably denied a student the opportunity to find a passion, a purpose, or a career pathway that could have changed the trajectory of their life. When a teacher speaks, students listen. And when a teacher communicates, even unintentionally, that certain pathways are beneath certain students, it reinforces a perception that's difficult to undo.

> ***If the adults in the room don't believe it, students won't choose it.***

If you've spent any time in a CTE classroom, you've heard it. A student drops into a seat on the first day, looks around, and says it without apology: "I didn't ask to be in this class. They just put me here."

It's said as a complaint. As a disclaimer. As a way of communicating that whatever happens in this room is not their fault and not their choice. And if you're the teacher on the receiving end of that statement, it can feel like a wall going up before the first lesson has even begun.

But here's what I want every CTE educator to hear: That student isn't the problem. That statement isn't a threat. It's an invitation, whether the student knows it or not. Because some of the most powerful CTE stories begin exactly that way. Not with a student who chose the pathway but with a student who was placed in it by someone who might not have even given it a second thought. Sometimes the most transformative moments in a student's life begin not with intention but with a scheduling decision.

It was the year 2000. A sophomore named Elizabeth Spell at West Brook High School in Beaumont, Texas, never planned to be in an agriculture class. She hadn't asked for it, hadn't researched it, hadn't considered it among her options. A counselor placed her there because the schedule required it. That was the extent of the decision-making.

What happened next is the part that should give every counselor, every advisor, and every education leader pause.

That student became her chapter's treasurer. She showed a heifer. She showed goats. She was breaking a mustang. She competed at the Fort Worth Livestock Show, at district leadership events, and at the Texas State FFA Convention. She won—Star Greenhand, Star Chapter, Equine Science, Livestock Judging, and Creed Speaking. And when asked about it, she said simply that she had developed leadership and a lot more self-confidence being in FFA.

An accident changed her life.

I never met Elizabeth Spell. But her story, documented in the West Brook High School yearbook in the year 2000, has stayed with me. Because it's not just her story. It's the story of every student who didn't ask to be in a CTE class yet found themselves there anyway.

Across every CTE classroom, in every school, in every district, there are students who didn't ask to be there. Students whose names landed on a roster because of a scheduling conflict, a filled elective, or a counselor who needed to place them somewhere. Students who walked in with no expectations and walked out with a direction they never saw coming. We don't always hear those stories. But they are happening every single day.

Now here's the harder question: How many students never get that accident? How many are guided—casually, quickly, without much thought—away from pathways that would have done the same thing? The counselor in that story didn't intend to change a trajectory. But the placement did. That's the weight of influence that sits in every scheduling conversation, every course recommendation, and every offhand comment made in a hallway between classes. When the adults in the building make decisions about where students belong, they're shaping futures whether they realize it or not.

That was twenty-six years ago. And the lesson hasn't changed.

Parents aren't the only ones who need to understand what CTE offers. The adults inside the building do, too. Because sometimes the most powerful thing a counselor can do for a student is to believe in a pathway before the student—or the parent—has been given any reason to.

The impact of staff mindset shows up in unexpected places. I remember reading a comment under one of our CTE Choice Awards videos from a teacher in a neighboring district who wrote publicly that they had only gone to Schooners, a local restaurant, to celebrate their CTE students. The comment was meant to be lighthearted, but it revealed something important: Even within the profession, CTE celebrations are sometimes treated as a social outing rather than recognition that goes above and beyond the status quo. Teachers need to feel validated. No one should come to work just to feel appreciated, but when you show them that you care, they'll show up for you. When leaders don't take CTE seriously, when CTE teachers feel unseen, students receive that signal long before they ever walk into a counselor's office. Mindset isn't just what we say in professional development sessions. It's what we say when we think no one is watching. It's how we celebrate CTE. It's how we tell our CTE story.

During one of our August professional development sessions, I told the CTE teachers that I needed to shift not just their understanding of their programs but their sense of professional worth. I told them directly, "You are just as important as core teachers. You've always been. The state holds us accountable for 40 percent of accountability, just like them." The room shifted. Not because the information was new but because someone in leadership had finally said it out loud, with conviction, in a room full of people who needed to hear it. When educators see themselves as important, they communicate that importance to students through their energy, their posture, and the pride they bring to their craft. And when students see that confidence reflected in their teachers, it reinforces their belief in the pathway.

Changing staff mindset is not only about what we say. It's also about how we present ourselves. I made a deliberate decision to brand our department in a way that communicated professional pride and identity. I looked at this from the lens of a high school principal: I needed to brand the department just like a high school is branded so that sense of connectedness was still there. People connect with things they can see, feel, and recognize as their own—a logo that represents them, colors that signal belonging, a motto that captures what they stand for. And if your department brand doesn't stand out, then you stand for nothing. We developed a logo, colors, and a motto. And then we held a *Real Housewives of Atlanta*-style professional photo and video shoot for our CTE team—the *Real Housewives* of CTE. Yes, a photo and video shoot. And I make no apologies for it. Because CTE needed to look like it took itself seriously. When our team showed up polished, unified, and proud, it sent a message to every principal, every counselor, and every student who encountered us: This department matters, and the people in it know it. You can't ask others to believe in something that you aren't visibly, publicly proud of yourself.

We also introduced CTE blazers and CTE shirts in our brand colors. It was a simple idea, but it carried real meaning. Just like football or basketball coaches on the sidelines of the field or court, we color coordinated our outfits with our CTE blazers for events, school board presentations, city council meetings, Chamber of Commerce meetings, community presentations, and special occasions. It created a sense of identity and belonging—a visible signal that this work was worth representing publicly. It showed that we are a team with one goal. And what happened next told me that something was shifting culturally:

Other departments in the district began adopting similar approaches. When I saw that, I thought, *Okay. That means something is moving.* You know you've built something worth noticing when others want to replicate it.

I also want to be honest about the leadership philosophy that guided how I built and maintained this team. My motto—written on a frame my sister bought from Kinkos and gave to me years ago—is simple: "Work hard, have fun, no drama." Those six words have guided more decisions than any strategic framework I have ever encountered. Work hard means you don't cut corners. Have fun means you bring energy to the work and celebrate what deserves celebrating. No drama means you stay focused on outcomes, not politics. When the people around you know what you stand for and how you operate, it creates a culture of trust. And trust is the foundation of every mindset shift.

None of this work happens alone. I was fortunate that when I became the director of CTE, I inherited a coordinator of CTE, Alicia Green, who had extensive experience and deep knowledge of accountability. She was a CTE counselor in Galena Park ISD in Houston, Texas, before coming to Beaumont ISD. I'll be honest: I was nervous at first. The coordinator of CTE position had been created before I became the director, which meant I didn't get to select my own person for that role. And I know firsthand how hard it is to move the needle with the wrong people on your team. But I quickly learned that I had nothing to worry about. I always knew when I was wrong about something because she would start off by saying, "Umm, Dr. Prudhomme," and right then I knew God had placed the right person on my team. That's the thing about leadership. Just because I was the director of CTE didn't mean I knew everything about CTE. I had just come from the role of high school principal, where English, math, science, and social studies were my priority. But working with Alicia put CTE on a fast pass to improvement because she can talk about CTE in her sleep. And she's the best coordinator a girl can have. When we met for the very first time, I knew we were a perfect fit. That foundation gave me something to build on.

As our work grew, I was able to create three new positions. I brought on Tanya Anderson as our coordinator of CTE instructional technology. I needed a person on my team who could handle all of our CTE technology needs. There's nothing more frustrating and nerve-wracking than having technical difficulties during IBC testing and waiting on the IT department to resolve it. What many people don't know is that Tanya and I go way back. We worked together at Clifton J. Ozen Magnet High School, where she was a CTE technology teacher. And she and her fellow teachers held down Long B Hall. There were no discipline problems in that hallway. None. That tells you everything you need to know about the kind of professional Tanya Anderson is. Tanya and I also share a similar background. We both came from the criminal justice system before finding our way into education. When I needed someone I could trust completely with our technology infrastructure, I didn't have to search. I already knew what Tanya was made of.

I brought on Eva LeBlanc as our coordinator of business and industry to meet with our business partners and community members, attend partnership meetings, and serve as someone who's plugged into industry so that CTE is always in the loop, they know what we do, and we are fulfilling the pipeline from school to work. What many people don't know is that Eva was my dance teacher and CCMR coordinator at Ozen High School before joining the CTE department. She's the person who dots every *i* and crosses every *t*. She never meets a stranger. She sees every situation with the glass half full. And she has exactly the kind of personality that thrives in the world of business and industry: warm, professional, relentless, and impossible not to trust. She doesn't tap dance around the issue (no pun intended). When I needed someone to be the face of CTE in rooms full of business executives and community leaders, I didn't have to look far. I already knew who she was.

And our CTE cheerleader, K–8 Career Readiness specialist Shamine Cormier—"whoop, whoop" as she says—educates our elementary and middle school students about CTE pathways and possibilities. I met Shamine in 2018 when she was leading the Jobs for America's Graduates (JAG) program at Central High School. The moment I encountered her energy, her creativity, and her ability to connect with people at every level, I knew immediately that she was the person to launch our new K–8 Career Readiness initiative. You can't put just anyone in a role that requires you to walk into an elementary school and make a kindergartner excited about a career pathway or walk into a middle school and convince a seventh grader that their future starts right now. It takes a special kind of person. Shamine is that person. And the "whoop, whoop" isn't just a catchphrase. It's who she is every single day.

I was also blessed that Dr. Allen reassigned one of my work besties, LaChandra Cobb-Eaglin, onto the team as our coordinator of STEM. She and I were assistant principals together at Ozen High School. LaChandra has a superpower when it comes to data. It's like she has the Midas touch when it comes to curriculum and instruction. I noticed this strength when we were assistant principals together, and I knew immediately that she was someone I could learn from. She can interpret data with her eyes closed. She has a strong leadership style, one that some people may misread as arrogance or feel threatened by. But she just knows her stuff. Period. When we were both high school principals, we shared ideas freely. There was no competition between us. Just two leaders who believed that when one of us got better, both of us got better.

With that team in place, we were complete. And when the former CTE Center principal retired, I remember Dr. Allen telling me that the new principal, Dr. Lori Threats, would be a good fit with our team. Dr. Threats came in with new ideas, listened to feedback, and opened the doors of the CTE Center wide. It's no longer the best-kept secret.

And behind every good leader is a good assistant. Stephanie Donald, our administrative assistant of CTE, is the person who keeps everything running quietly, consistently, and without fanfare. She's the first voice people hear when they call our department. She's the one making sure the details are handled so the rest of us can focus on the work. A team is only as strong as the people holding it together behind the scenes, and Stephanie has been holding ours together from the very beginning.

Having the right people sitting at your table changes everything. Not just because of what they know but because of how they show up. They push you. They challenge your thinking. They carry the mission when the weight gets heavy. They celebrate the wins with you. And on the days when the perception problem feels too entrenched to move, they remind you why you started. My dad always told me that you're only as good as the people you surround yourself with. He was right. I always say, "Have the right people sitting at your table because the work is too important to do with the wrong ones."

The structure of our department reflects the philosophy behind it. Each member of my team owns specific programs of study, not as a title but as a real form of accountability. Eva LeBlanc oversees Agriculture, Construction, Cosmetology, Law, Maritime, Real Estate, JROTC, and Teaching and Training programs—the business and industry connections that tie each of those pathways to real workforce opportunities. LaChandra Cobb-Eaglin oversees Architectural Drafting, Business and Entrepreneurship, Engineering, and Transportation—the STEM and career pathway programs that connect students to the industries driving Southeast Texas. Tanya Anderson oversees Digital Communications, Graphic Design, Computer Science, Culinary Arts, Health Science, and Welding—ensuring that every teacher in those programs has the technology support and instructional resources they need. Shamine Cormier owns the entire Middle School portfolio—more than twenty middle school teachers whose students are the future pipeline for every program we offer at the high school level. As coordinator of CTE, Alicia owns the full academic and accountability infrastructure of the department—Lamar

Institute of Technology (LIT)/Lamar State College-Orange (LSCO) dual enrollment, CTE course scheduling, iCEV curriculum, counselor liaison, Eduthings, teacher information sheets, teacher certification lists, teacher master schedules, industry-based certification teacher assignment lists, IBC software orders, IBC reimbursements, CTSOs, and the CCMR Strategic Team. That isn't a job description. That's a command center. When I say she can talk about CTE in her sleep, this list is what I mean. She isn't just knowledgeable about CTE. She is the operational backbone of everything that keeps it running. This isn't a department held together by good intentions. It's a department held together by structure, accountability, and the right people in the right roles.

This structure is built on a simple but powerful principle: Put your position where the points lie. When each coordinator is aligned to specific programs of study, the accountability becomes clear and direct. The person overseeing the program owns the data that comes from it. They know the IBC pass rates. They know the enrollment numbers. They know where the gaps are and where the growth is happening. There's no ambiguity about who is responsible for what. And when something isn't working, there's no confusion about who needs to address it. Accountability without alignment is just blame. But when your team structure mirrors your program structure—when the person at the table is the same person responsible for the outcomes—accountability becomes productive. It becomes a tool for growth rather than a source of conflict. Put your position where the points lie. And then trust the people in those positions to own what they're responsible for.

Having the right people at the table isn't enough if those people don't have a voice. My team and I meet monthly for our CTE huddle meetings, a dedicated space where every person on the team is heard. Each team member has a spot on the rolling agenda—their own standing place to bring updates, raise concerns, share wins, and contribute to the direction of the work. It's important for the people sitting at your table to know that their seat means something. That they weren't just placed there to receive information but to contribute to it. As the leader, you have to be ready to listen—really listen—not just to respond but to learn. Because the people closest to the work often see what the leader can't see from the top. And if you build a table where people feel safe to speak, you'll never have to wonder what's really happening in your department. They will tell you.

Not every huddle looks the same. In December, our monthly huddle becomes the Holiday Huddle. We meet at a local restaurant and exchange Christmas gifts and share in a White Elephant gift exchange. It's not a meeting with an agenda. It's a celebration of the people at the table and the year we've built together. And our final huddle of the year is our End of Year Retreat held off campus, away from the building, away from the emails, away from the daily demands of the work. It's a dedicated space to reflect on what we've accomplished, what we've learned, and what we're carrying into the next year. Culture isn't built only in the hard moments. It's built in the moments when you stop, step away from the work, and remind the people around you that they matter beyond what they produce. Those gatherings aren't optional. They're essential.

Structure without a plan is just good intentions. That's why every member of our CTE team operates from a CTE Year at a Glance—a month-by-month planning document that maps out the full scope of their responsibilities from August through June. Each team member has their own individualized version tailored to their specific role and program assignments. But the framework is shared. Because when everyone on the team is working from the same calendar structure, the work stays coordinated, deadlines don't get missed, and no one is caught off guard by what's coming next. From budget timelines and Perkins grant deadlines to CTE Month activities, IBC testing windows, pre-registration season, advisory council meetings, and the CTE Choice Awards—

everything lives on the calendar. The Year at a Glance isn't just a planning tool. It's a culture document. It says that in this department, we plan ahead, we stay organized, and we show up prepared. Every single month.

This is also why I'm not too proud to learn from others. If I hear about a strong CTE program in another district, we go see it. I take my team, get in our CTE vehicles, and go learn. We walk through their facility, talk with their staff, and come back with ideas we can adapt and make our own. That experience reinforces something I believe deeply: There's always something to learn. And when leaders model that kind of humility and curiosity—when they're willing to say "Show me what you're doing so I can do it better"—it creates a culture where growth is valued rather than threatened.

One of the most memorable examples of this was when I loaded up my CTE team and we made the drive to Houston to visit the WorkTexas Trade School at Gallery Furniture. When we heard about what "Mattress Mack" Jim McIngvale, the owner of Gallery Furniture, had built inside his retail store, we had to see it for ourselves: a fully functioning trade school offering training in carpentry, construction, welding, culinary arts, and auto mechanics, with free daycare so that parents could learn without worrying about their children. It was unconventional. It was creative. And it was working. We walked through that space as a team and came back to Beaumont with something no professional development session could have given us: a reminder that the pathways we're building for our students are the same pathways that adults across Houston are lining up to access.

When more than 3,000 people inquire about a trade school inside a furniture store, that isn't a trend. That's a confirmation. The skills we teach matter. The certifications we offer open doors. And if Mattress Mack understood that—and built an entire school around it inside his own building—then we had every reason to keep building ours.

When staff mindset shifts, everything begins to align. Counselors present options with clarity and confidence. Teachers reinforce the value of different pathways. Leaders make decisions that reflect a broader understanding of success. And students respond. Because at the end of the day, students aren't just choosing programs. They're responding to what the adults around them believe. And when those adults believe—truly believe—everything else begins to move.

You can't change perception without the right people in the classroom. And right now 31 percent of schools across the country struggle to fill CTE teacher positions.[4] Nearly one in three schools can't find qualified CTE teachers. That isn't a funding problem alone. That's a perception problem. When a career field isn't seen as prestigious or valued, the pipeline of people willing to enter it shrinks. The same stigma that follows students into CTE classrooms follows teachers away from them.

I was sitting in a coffee shop recently when a parent approached me. She told me her daughter was interested in engineering and wanted to attend the career center her junior year. I asked if her daughter had taken any engineering classes. She said no. I asked why. She told me the counselor had advised her daughter that those classes weren't important enough for her to take.

This wasn't a new counselor finding her footing. This was a veteran counselor. Someone with years of experience. Someone students and families trusted. And without realizing it—without any malice, without any intention to harm—she had used her position and her credibility to direct a student away from engineering before that student ever had the chance to try it.

That isn't a counselor problem. That's a perception problem. And it happened today. In 2026. In our own schools.

---

4 National Center for Education Statistics, "Condition of Education 2024," Institute of Education Sciences, May 2024, https://ies.ed.gov/learn/press-release/ncess-condition-education-sheds-light-enrollment-trends-early-childhood-k-12-and-postsecondary.

PART 03

OWNERSHIP & AWARENESS

The Story Behind the Shift

CHAPTER 7

FROM TEACHER TO DIRECTOR —WHAT I SAW DIDN'T CHANGE

My lived experience across time

I remember my parents asking me what I wanted to major in. My dad wanted to be a teacher, and he tried to talk me into majoring in education. I didn't want to. I was undecided for a while, pulled between general business and occupational therapy, before finding my way to the path that felt right. My dad saw something in me that I hadn't yet seen in myself. But at that age, you don't always recognize wisdom when it's standing right in front of you wearing your dad's face. I chose criminal justice instead, and that decision led me exactly where I was supposed to go—right back to the classroom my dad always knew I belonged in. He wasn't wrong about education. Because here I am.

I always wanted to be a prison warden. I'm not entirely sure how I landed there, but my bachelor's degree was in criminal justice, and in the early 1990s, the prison system in Texas was booming. My career began in 1994 as a district parole officer and substance abuse counselor in both a state prison and a federal prison. I entered that work with purpose. I believed in rehabilitation. I believed people could change.

But something started to disturb me. I kept seeing the same faces. Young people—too young—cycling through those doors again and again. The revolving door was real, and it was relentless. After four years of watching it, I knew I couldn't stay. I remember sitting in my office one day, genuinely wrestling with a question: What role can I play to change this? Because seeing them in here, I realized, was already too late.

I will never forget the day I called the Beaumont ISD's job line and heard that there was a criminal justice vacancy at my high school alma mater. I sat up immediately. I called the school, made an appointment with the principal—Terry Ingram, who had been my own high school principal—and received a callback for an interview. He recommended me for hire. I remember feeling a deep sense of relief as I submitted my resignation. I felt I could do more good on the other side of those prison doors.

My resignation was not well received. I had just returned from two weeks of mandatory job training in Glynco, Georgia. Dr. Jim Mann told me the government had invested in my background check and training, and that quitting after only six months of being on this job meant I wouldn't be welcomed back to the Federal Bureau of Prisons. He said people don't quit jobs like this. I told him I wanted to work toward my doctorate and dedicate myself to working with young people so they wouldn't position themselves to live a life behind prison doors. My decision was made.

I'm a Beaumont ISD product. I attended Blanchette Elementary School grades K–3, Price Elementary School fourth and fifth grade, Vincent Middle School, and graduated from West Brook High School in 1990. The community I now serve is the community that shaped me. The schools I now work with are the schools that gave me my foundation. When I walked back through those doors as a CTE teacher, I wasn't just starting a career. I was coming home. And when I eventually became the director of CTE for the same district that educated me,

I understood in a deeply personal way what was at stake. These weren't just students. They were me, thirty years earlier, standing at the same crossroads, needing the same thing I had needed: someone to believe in the pathway in front of them and tell them it was worth choosing.

I began my journey in education in 1998 as a CTE teacher—entering the profession with a strong sense of purpose, a belief in the power of education to change lives, and a belief that schools were places where every student could find a path forward.

I'll be honest about those first days in the classroom. Nobody told me it would feel like that. I had come straight from industry. I knew criminal justice, I believed in the work, I had purpose. But I had no pedagogy. No student teaching experience. No frame of reference for what it actually felt like to stand in front of six or seven periods of students every single day and be responsible for all of it.

It almost took me out. Those sixth and seventh period classes almost gave me gray hair.

I remember going home and telling my husband I couldn't do this. And he looked at me and said, "You have to. You already quit your other job."

He was right. So, I stayed. And what carried me through wasn't a training program or a professional development session. It was the people in the building who had been doing this work and knew what a new teacher needed: CTE department head Eileen Slater. Theo Thomas. Sandra Williams. Jean Bryant. And Patrick Calhoun, the director of CTE at the time, who supported new CTE teachers and understood what it meant to come from industry into the classroom without a traditional teaching background. They were my lifeline. They answered my questions, shared their strategies, talked me through the hard days, and reminded me by their example that this work was possible—

and worth doing. I wouldn't have survived that first year without them. And I wouldn't have become the educator I am without what they poured into me.

There's something I want CTE teachers to understand, something that took me years to fully articulate but that I knew intuitively from the first day I stood in front of a classroom. As a CTE teacher, you have advantages that core teachers don't always have. I'm not saying that to start a competition. It's not us versus them. I'm saying it because I want you to see what you're holding. You have tools. You have industry connections. You have content that is inherently hands-on, inherently relevant, and inherently connected to the real world. You have the freedom to be as creative and inventive as you want to be. And when you use that freedom fully, students show up differently.

I know this because I lived it.

When I was a criminal justice teacher, I had a classroom set of twenty-five textbooks. I refused to let my class be about vocabulary and worksheets. I brought in correctional officers. I brought in community professionals who could speak to what the justice system actually looked like from the inside. And one time I brought in an inmate.

In 1999, I had the opportunity to visit the High School for Law and Justice in Houston, formerly the High School for Law Enforcement and Criminal Justice. I went with Dr. Carrol Thomas, who was the superintendent at the time, along with the assistant superintendent, Beth Fischenich; the principal, Terry Ingram; and the director of CTE, Patrick Calhoun. I came back with more ideas than my budget could handle and more inspiration than my portable classroom had room to store.

That visit changed everything about how I taught. I began holding mock trials in the master teacher room. Every student had a role. Every role had a costume. My student officers wore police shirts with holsters and rubber simulated guns.

Students played the judge, the attorneys, the witnesses, and the defendant, all the way down to the inmate on trial. It was real. It was rigorous. And it was CTE doing exactly what it's supposed to do.

I still remember the knock at my door from a Beaumont Police Department officer working security that day. He had followed one of my students to class because he genuinely thought a student was impersonating a police officer. That's how real it was.

Every year, I took my underclassmen to the local courthouse and jails. I took my seniors on their senior field trip to the Houston courthouse and jail. It was one of the most meaningful experiences I could offer them, and I made sure it was done right. I chartered a bus from Honey Charter Service. And my dad, true to who he has always been, made sure he was there himself as the driver.

When I left in 2001, the teacher who took my place told me she had lost count of how many times the classroom door swung open with students asking, "Where is Mrs. Prudhomme?"

One of the most impactful moments of my career as a CTE educator came years after I had left that classroom. Former students reached out to tell me they had majored in criminal justice in college because of me. Not because of a textbook. Not because of a test. Because of what happened in that classroom—the mock trials, the field trips, the correction officers, the real conversations about what the justice system actually looked like from the inside.

They chose a career pathway because a teacher believed in it enough to bring it to life. That's the power of a CTE teacher who uses everything they've been given. That's the moment I understood that the work we do in CTE classrooms doesn't end when the bell rings. It follows students into their futures.

That's what happens when a CTE teacher uses everything they've been given.

And the connection runs even deeper than West Brook. I was the principal at Ozen High School, a place where I once walked the halls as a student at the West Brook Ninth Grade Center. That building held history long before it held me. My father and my sisters graduated from Hebert High School—the blue and gold Panthers. Ozen had the same colors and the same mascot. As principal, I adopted their motto: "Whatever Hebert does must be the best." It was simple yet unshakeable. That standard—that belief that excellence isn't optional, that whatever you put your name on must represent the best of who you are—was woven into the fabric of my family long before I ever stood at the front of a classroom or behind a principal's desk. When I became the principal of the school that occupied that same space, I felt the weight of that history. And I carried it with me every single day.

Before there was a CTE Choice Awards, there were two events happening at Ozen High School that nobody had asked for and nobody could ignore.

Camille Briggs, our Video Technology teacher, was a go-getter. She went into the community and secured sponsorships from local businesses so that the majority of her students could travel to California, more than 1,500 miles from Beaumont. She made that trip four years in a row and took them to New York—over 1,700 miles away—one year. Through her program, Panther Productions, students visited Universal Studios and UCLA, toured film schools, and experienced life outside of Southeast Texas in ways that most of them never had before. They saw things they wouldn't have gotten a chance to see anywhere else. As an assistant principal, I traveled to California with her students twice.

I remember one of those California trips when Camille had to take a test to become an Apple Certified Trainer so that her students could earn Final Cut Pro certifications. She didn't do it on her own time, in her own city. She did it on a trip she'd already organized, funded through community sponsorships, and traveled thousands of miles to lead. And I want to be clear about the context: This was before industry-based certifications were even a requirement for CTE. Nobody was asking her to certify her students. Nobody asked her to go to California as her end-of-the-year trip for her senior students. There was no accountability measure demanding it. There was no cord to wear at graduation. She did it because she understood, long before the system caught up, that a credential recognized by an industry was worth more than a classroom grade. That isn't dedication. That's vision. That's a teacher who saw the future of CTE before anyone had written it into policy.

The trips became so popular that Camille took it a step further. She created the Ozen Grammys, an annual Grammy-style red carpet awards show specifically for her Video Technology students. She built the experience. And the students came. Because that's what happens when a teacher believes so completely in her students that she creates something worthy of them: They show up for it.

I took that same belief and expanded it to the entire school. Ozen hosted its first Oscars ceremony in the Ozen band hall, an invite-only academic celebration. They walked the red carpet. Awards were presented. A spaghetti lunch was served. It wasn't a pep rally. It wasn't a standard school assembly. It was a deliberate celebration designed to communicate one thing: Your achievement is worth honoring in a room that feels worthy of it.

Neither of these events was in anyone's job description. Both required a willingness to step outside the box because we believed our students deserved a moment that matched the size of what they'd accomplished.

The road to this role was shaped by more than years of experience. It was shaped by crisis. In 2017, Hurricane Harvey caused severe water damage and extensive mold growth at Central High School. LaChandra Cobb-Eaglin was principal at Central at the time, and I was principal at Ozen. We were colleagues navigating the same storm, literally and figuratively. In January

2018, the BISD board of managers made the decision to close Central High School. The two campuses merged to form Beaumont United High School, with the new school operating on the former Ozen campus. For six months, LaChandra and I took on dual roles: maintaining stability and composure for our own campus communities while simultaneously working to help build an entirely new high school from the ground up. That isn't something they teach in a leadership program. That's something you learn by living through it.

What most people didn't see was what that merger cost us personally. I wrote this Facebook post in the midst of it, and I share it here because it captures something that no professional summary ever could:

> *This has been a very challenging school year for Beaumont ISD. But it will be ok. My career at Ozen began in 2003. I have held the positions of counselor, assistant principal, interim principal —and I will be the last principal of Clifton J. Ozen Magnet High School. Wow. I still cannot believe it, but it will be ok. It is hard to believe that 3443 Fannett Road will have a new name, new colors, and a new mascot in August, but it will be ok. Mrs. LaChandra Cobb-Eaglin and I worked together at Ozen and we are very good friends. We have shared ideas, plans, and projects with each other for many years. We have learned from each other and will continue to do so. You just do not know how hard this has been for both of us. Mrs. Cobb-Eaglin and I have spent countless days and hours crying, praying, venting, supporting, and encouraging each other. And sometimes—we laugh just to keep from crying. As the leaders, we have to be strong for our students and staff to make this transition smooth for them. But in reality, we are trying to be strong for us. To my faculty, staff, and student body at Ozen High School—we will be ok. No more Ozen and Central rivalry. We are family now. We*

> *have to show love over hate. Have faith over fear. We have to let go of the past and cherish the memories. It will be ok.*
>
> — **Dr. Donna Prudhomme,**
> Proud Ozen High School Principal

The merger was hard. But what made it bearable was knowing what it had meant to the students who walked those halls. I still have a card from a student named Kobe D. that captures everything I was feeling in that season and everything I hoped my leadership had meant:

> *A truly amazing principal is hard to find, difficult to part with, and impossible to forget. Thank you for being Ozen's greatest administrator ever. I wish you nothing but the best in your future occupation.*
>
> *You taught me so much more than books ever could. Thanks for an amazing high school experience, Dr. Prudhomme.*
>
> — **Kobe D.,** Ozen Student

That card lives in my office. It has moved with me from Ozen to the district office. On the days when the work feels thankless, when the perception problem feels too entrenched to move, I read it. And I remember why none of this is about a title or an award. It's about what a student believes about themselves when they leave your building.

Leadership isn't just what you do in the building. It's what you carry when the building closes. And sometimes the most honest thing a leader can say is exactly what I said that day: It will be okay. Not because everything is fine. But because you've decided—in the middle of the hardest thing—that you're going to believe it anyway.

After Ozen closed and Beaumont United was established, I was promoted to director of Career and Technical Education, and the work that had been personal for so long became my full-time mission. The merger was done. Beaumont United was established. It was time to build. What I didn't know was that the disruptions were just beginning. Look at what the first eight years of this work actually looked like:

- 2017–2018: Hurricane Harvey
- 2018–2019: The merger. Two schools becoming one.
- 2019–2020: Tropical Storm Imelda in the fall. A global pandemic in the spring.
- 2020–2021: A full year of virtual learning.
- 2021–2022: The year after COVID-19, running an eight-period block schedule trying to recover what students had lost.
- 2022–2023: Another eight-period schedule. Still recovering.
- 2023–2024: Transition to a seven-period schedule.
- 2024–2025: Seven-period schedule.
- 2025–2026: Seven-period schedule.

In 2021, I was approached about applying for an assistant superintendent position. On paper, it was the next logical step. The superintendent credential was there. The experience was there. But I wasn't there, not in the way that role required.

I was still grieving. I had lost my parents. I had lost my sister. Three losses that came closer together than any person should have to carry. I could barely keep it together. I knew what I was capable of. But I also knew that sitting at that table—at that level, with that weight—required a version of me that I hadn't yet found my way back to. So, I said no. Not because I didn't belong there. But because I knew myself well enough to know that the timing wasn't right. Grief has its own schedule. And leadership requires you to be present in ways that loss doesn't always allow.

I don't regret that decision. I regret the losses that made it necessary.

Not one of those years was normal. Not one. And yet, in the middle of every single one of them, we kept building. We kept certifying students. We kept telling the story. We kept showing up. Because the work doesn't pause for a hurricane. It doesn't pause for a pandemic. And it doesn't pause for a schedule change. The students still needed us. And we were still there.

It was Roland Antoine, then associate principal at West Brook High School and later principal at Ozen High School, who hired me as a counselor—a role that would open my eyes to how deeply perception shaped the choices students were making every single day.

As a counselor, I sat with students who dismissed the CTE Center before they understood what it offered. They had already decided what attending there would say about them. As a high school assistant principal and then high school principal, I saw how scheduling decisions communicated priority without anyone intending to. CTE was included in the schedule, but it wasn't always positioned with the same weight as other offerings. CTE accomplishments were present, but they weren't always elevated in the same spaces as academic achievements. That difference mattered—because what is celebrated becomes what is valued, and what is valued becomes what is pursued.

Even when I stepped away from the day-to-day work, I couldn't fully step away from the mission. Whether I was on the road or sitting still for a moment, my mind kept returning to the same questions: What are other districts doing? What could we do differently? What would it take to change what people believe about CTE? That's not unusual for educators who care deeply. But it told me something important: This work had become more than professional. It had become personal because I had lived the pattern from inside it, at every level.

By the time I stepped into the role of director of Career and Technical Education in 2018, I had experienced the system from multiple perspectives. I expected that, at the district level, I would see a different picture. And in many ways, I did. Programs were stronger, pathways were more aligned with industry, opportunities were expanding in exciting ways. But there was one thing that hadn't changed: perception. The same patterns I had observed as a teacher were still present. The same stigma I had seen as a high school counselor still existed. The same structural challenges I had navigated as a high school principal were still influencing decisions.

During my first year as director of CTE, I remember Alicia Green and I meeting with Dr. Ron Jackson, the principal of Beaumont United High School, to discuss his CTE program. In that conversation, he said something that stayed with me. He told me that when he was principal at Central, no one had ever explained CTE to him the way we did. That statement said everything. Here was a principal—an experienced school leader—who had overseen a campus with CTE programs and had never received a clear, compelling explanation of what those programs were, what they offered, or why they mattered. That wasn't his failure. That was a visibility failure. And it confirmed what I was already beginning to understand: the perception problem wasn't just with students and parents. It lived inside the system itself, at every level, including in the offices of the very principals responsible for championing CTE on their campuses.

The programs hadn't failed the students. The narrative had.

That realization was both frustrating and clarifying. Frustrating because it meant that despite all the progress, something essential hadn't shifted.

Clarifying because it helped me understand where the real work needed to be done. The issue wasn't the programs. The issue wasn't the opportunities. The issue was how those programs and opportunities were being seen. And once I saw that clearly, I couldn't unsee it. It's a story about perception. A story about how students are guided. A story about how systems communicate value. And once you see that story, you're responsible for changing it.

When I took over as director of CTE and began looking at Career and Technical Education through a different pair of lenses, something became clear very quickly. We stood alone. It felt like we didn't fit in. Like we had been left out of conversations that every other department was part of—conversations that shaped the entire direction of the school year before it ever began.

Summer school planning meetings happened without us—because CTE summer programs were never held. Summer curriculum planning happened without us—because CTE classes were considered electives. Core curriculum got a seat at the table. Fine arts got a seat. Physical education got a seat. But CTE did not. Nobody said we weren't welcome. Nobody sent a memo that said CTE doesn't belong here. We were simply not included. And in a system, being left out of the room is its own kind of message. It communicates, without a single word, that what you do isn't important enough to plan for.

That's not a scheduling oversight. That's a perception problem. And it was sitting right at the center of the district's own internal structures. It had been this way for years. And when I finally named the root cause, it came down to one thing: visibility.

The lesson didn't come from an education conference or a curriculum guide. It came from the world of business branding. Ryan Serhant, one of the most recognized names in real estate and the author of *Brand It Like Serhant*, built his career on a simple principle: If people don't see it, it doesn't exist. He was talking about real estate. But that truth translates directly into education. Programs that students don't see, don't choose, and don't understand will never be valued. Departments that aren't in the room when decisions are made won't be represented in the decisions that come out of that room. CTE had been doing the work. But the work was invisible. And invisible work doesn't change minds, doesn't fill seats, and doesn't earn the kind of institutional respect that translates into a seat at the planning table.

That's when I understood that visibility wasn't a marketing strategy. It was a survival strategy. And it had to start with me.

CHAPTER 8

"STAY VISIBLE" —THE LEADERSHIP SHIFT

The move from campus to district—and what changed

I still think about something that happened during my teacher evaluation training. The presenter, David Hicks, held up a book and said this was everything you needed to know about leadership. Then he flipped through the pages. They were blank. Every single page. He was making a point that has stayed with me ever since: that leadership isn't something handed to you. It's something you build. And in education, we have too often treated the most important work as if someone else already wrote the book on it. They didn't. We're still writing it. And Career and Technical Education has paid the price for that assumption for decades.

The transition from campus leadership to district leadership isn't simply a change in role. It's a shift in how influence works, how impact is measured, and how visibility is created. What felt immediate and tangible at the campus level becomes broader and, at times, more abstract at the district level. The work changes, and so must the approach to leadership.

When I became the director of Career and Technical Education, I quickly realized that the way I had led as a high school principal would not fully translate into this new role. As a high school principal, visibility was built into the position. I was present in the building every day, interacting with students, teachers, and staff constantly. I was part of the daily rhythm of the school. At the district level, that visibility doesn't happen automatically. It has to be created, sustained, and protected.

My assistant superintendent, Dr. Allen, who had been my mentor for several years and later became superintendent, told me early on, "You have to stay visible." At the time, I nodded, but I didn't fully understand what she meant. I had always been visible. But what I came to understand is that visibility at the district level isn't about presence. It's about intentionality. It's something you have to architect deliberately. And more importantly, I began to realize that it wasn't just about my visibility. It was about the visibility of Career and Technical Education itself.

> ***Visibility isn't a byproduct of good work. It's a leadership responsibility.***

The perception problem didn't build itself overnight. It took decades. It took legislation. It took systems and structures and casual comments in hallways and counseling sessions that directed students away without anyone realizing what they were doing. That narrative has had a long head start. And you can't whisper your way past it. You have to be intentional. You have to be consistent. You have to be visible in rooms where CTE was never invited. You have to tell the story before someone else tells the wrong one. CTE has to be louder than the stigma that preceded it. Not louder in volume. Louder in presence. Louder in data. Louder in celebration. Louder in every room where decisions are made about what students deserve to believe about their future.

Everything we built as a department was designed with visibility in mind. The logo, the colors, the motto, the blazers, the photo and video shoot—none of it was decoration. All of it was communication. We'd already done that work, and I could see the results: Other departments were replicating our approach, our team carried themselves differently, and students and principals began to recognize the CTE brand as something worth paying attention to. But branding alone was not enough. Visibility requires consistent, sustained presence in every space where decisions about students are being made.

Our vision was "to become an educational leader in delivering real-world learning and experiences that prepare students to effectively transition into postsecondary and career opportunities." Our mission was "to graduate students with industry certifications, licenses, postsecondary certificates, and degrees to equip and position them to enter the workforce and/or become entrepreneurs." Those weren't words we put on a flyer. They were the foundation everything else was built on.

Our motto, slogan, and theme—"Preparing for the *REAL* world in a *REAL* way," "Be College, Career, or Military READY," and "Future Ready"—weren't chosen casually. Every word is intentional. "REAL" means something. "Future Ready" means something. And when students see those words on a blazer, a banner, or a social media post, they're receiving a message about what this department believes about them.

One of the first things I discovered when I stepped into the director role was that February is CTE Month nationally. Our district didn't know this. There was no campaign, no recognition, no intentional effort to use that month as a platform for elevating Career and Technical Education. I made sure that changed immediately. This is what I mean when I say you have to toot your own horn. In education, there's sometimes an unspoken belief that good work should speak for itself—that if your programs are strong, people will notice.

But that's not how perception works. Perception is shaped by what is amplified. If you're doing remarkable things and you aren't telling anyone, you aren't being humble.

You're being invisible. And invisible programs don't attract students, don't earn community support, and don't change how people think about Career and Technical Education. Visibility is an act of advocacy. Every announcement, every social media post, every press release, every recognition moment is a message that says, "This work matters, these students matter, and this department is worth your attention."

Staying visible also meant owning how our story was told digitally. BISDTV, our district's digital communications platform, is led by CTE teachers at our high schools, with student workers who are trained on the A/V equipment. When we have big events, BISDTV is there to capture it. Those students aren't just filming. They're learning broadcast journalism, production, and media communication in real time through a CTE program. And then we took it a step further: We began livestreaming our football games on the CTE YouTube channel.

That decision was about more than sports. It was about training our student workers on A/V equipment. It was about reach. It was about making sure that when families, community members, and industry partners tuned in, they were doing so through a CTE platform.

Every viewer became an audience for our story. The goal was simple: If we were doing remarkable things, the world needed to see them in real time. We weren't going to wait for someone else to tell our story. We were going to tell it ourselves—consistently, unapologetically, and on every platform available to us.

Visibility isn't always about stages and ceremonies. Sometimes it shows up in the smallest moments—a hallway conversation, a quick check-in, a simple question. I kept a letter from a student named T. Booker that reminds me of this every time I read it:

> *Dr. P, thank you for helping me this year. You took a big chance with me. You don't know how it made me feel for you to ask me "Am I ok?" or "Do I need anything." You made me feel special here. And I hate that you are leaving me. But I know I'm going to be ok because I know you are going to pop up and surprise us. Thank you for being there when I need someone.*
>
> — **T. Booker.,** Ozen Student

That letter isn't about programs or data or accountability metrics. It's about a student who needed someone to see them. And the most visible thing I ever did at Ozen had nothing to do with a press release. It was asking a student if they were okay—and meaning it.

I remember the previous CTE Center principal always saying the CTE Center was the best-kept secret. I never understood why he was so proud of that. If it's so good, then why is it a secret? A secret isn't a compliment. A secret is a visibility failure. And visibility failures cost students opportunities they never knew existed. Never say "Shh, it's a secret." Tell your CTE story.

Looking back, the advice to "stay visible" meant far more than I initially understood. It wasn't just about being present. It was about ensuring that Career and Technical Education was seen, understood, and valued in every space where decisions were being made. It was about leading in a way that made the invisible visible. Because once people can see it—really see it—they begin to believe it. And belief is where everything starts.

CHAPTER 9

THE MOMENT I REALIZED PERCEPTION WAS THE PROBLEM

My turning point

There are moments in leadership that don't arrive all at once. They build quietly, piece by piece, until something shifts and you can finally see clearly what was always there. What once felt like a series of unrelated challenges begins to form a pattern. What once seemed like isolated situations reveals itself as something much deeper and more systemic.

For me, the realization that perception was the problem didn't come from a single event. It came from a series of moments that, over time, began to point unmistakably in the same direction. For years, I had addressed each situation as its own challenge. A student hesitant to enroll in a CTE course felt like a counseling issue. A scheduling conflict felt like a structural problem. A parent pulling their child from a program felt like a communication failure. A teacher making a dismissive comment about certain pathways felt like a mindset problem to be corrected individually.

Each situation seemed separate. But it wasn't.

I began to think about the patterns I'd seen across my entire career. I thought about the stigma that followed the CTE Center when I was a high school counselor—a stigma nobody had written down, nobody had formally taught, but everybody somehow knew. I thought about the parents who removed their children from CTE programs year after year, not because the programs were ineffective but because they didn't trust what those programs would lead to. I thought about the student who was told she was "too strong" academically for CTE—a statement that redirected her path based entirely on what someone believed the pathway represented, not what it actually offered.

The turning point wasn't a single moment. It was the moment I stopped seeing isolated problems and started seeing one systemic truth.

And then I stepped back. I stopped looking at each situation individually, and I started asking a different question: What do all of these moments have in common? The answer became clear: perception. Every one of these situations was rooted not in what was true about Career and Technical Education but in what people believed about it. Students believed certain pathways meant certain things about them. Parents believed certain choices led to certain outcomes. Educators believed, however unconsciously, that certain students belonged in certain spaces. And those beliefs were driving decisions at every level of the system.

In 2023, my colleagues nominated me for the Career & Technical Association of Texas (CTAT) Administrator of the Year award. It was one of the most meaningful nominations I had received—not because of the recognition itself but because of what it represented. The people who worked alongside me, who had watched this work unfold from the inside, believed it was worth honoring.

When I was nominated for the CTAT Administrator of the Year, Jenny Angelo, executive director of curriculum and instruction for Beaumont ISD—

the person who directly oversaw our department—wrote a letter of support to the award committee. In that letter she described Operation IBC, the CTE Choice Awards, and the business and industry partnerships we'd built: the maritime pathway at the Port of Beaumont, the STEM partnerships with ExxonMobil and OCI, the healthcare, HVAC, automotive, and culinary placements across Southeast Texas. She wrote that each of these changes had profoundly impacted students, the community, and the workforce of Southeast Texas. And she said that my contributions to the district and community exceeded the award criteria. That letter changed something for me. Not because of what it said about an award. But because of what it said about the work. When the person responsible for overseeing your department puts her name on a letter and tells a state committee that what you built is worthy of recognition—that's the system beginning to see what you always believed was there. That's the perception beginning to shift from the inside out.

The following February, my coworkers and I made the drive to San Antonio for the CTAT Winter Conference and the in-person interviews. It was a panel of CTE teachers and leaders—people who understood this world, who lived in it the same way I did. I knew what I needed to do. I told my story. I talked about branding the department, about looking through the lens of a high school principal who understands how a school's identity shapes everything that happens inside it, about how I knew from the beginning that the real work was changing the mindset of students, parents, teachers, and staff. Not just improving programs but changing what people believe about them.

At the conclusion of my interview, something happened that I wasn't expecting. Several of the interviewers said, almost in unison, "By the way, it's not just you. We're all dealing with the same thing in our districts."

I'll admit that made me feel better than I expected it to. Because leadership can be isolating. You can spend years fighting for something you believe in, wondering if the resistance you face is particular to your situation or part of something much larger. In that room, I got my answer. The perception problem wasn't unique to my district. It wasn't a reflection of something I'd done wrong. It was a systemic reality that CTE leaders across the country were navigating every day—often without the language to name it, often without knowing that others were standing in the same place they were.

I left that interview feeling like I hadn't impressed the panel. I had told my truth, but I was uncertain whether my truth had landed the way I hoped. Months passed. I assumed the award had gone to someone else, and I moved forward.

Then Robin Painovich, the executive director of CTAT, called. I had won. I was named the 2024 CTAT Administrator of the Year. I then went on to compete at the regional level alongside exceptional CTE leaders from Arkansas, Louisiana, New Mexico, and Oklahoma—and was named the 2025 Association for Career and Technical Education (ACTE) Region IV Administrator of the Year. I was surprised.

While I knew other districts in Texas were facing similar CTE challenges, I didn't think my story would resonate at the regional level the way it had at the state level. But it did. And then came the national level. To compete as one of five national finalists alongside leaders from Alabama, Indiana, Michigan, and Arizona, I told myself the same thing I'd told myself from the beginning: Keep telling your story. And it worked.

After eight years of fighting for CTE—processing the no's, explaining over and over what CTE was and why we needed this or that, the glaring looks that said "It's just CTE," the silence that was sometimes construed as "You're not important"—that three-year process of interviewing and telling our story had resonated. At every level. From district to region to national.

The following is the official press release from ACTE:

FOR IMMEDIATE RELEASE

December 11, 2025

ACTE Announces Texas Director of Career and Technical Education as the 2026 National Award Winner

ALEXANDRIA, VA—Today, the Association for Career and Technical Education (ACTE) announced Dr. Donna Prudhomme, Director of Career and Technical Education (CTE) at Beaumont ISD in Beaumont, TX as the 2026 ACTE Administrator of the Year – National Winner. This award recognizes administrative CTE professionals at the school, district, county, state, or federal level who have demonstrated leadership in ensuring teacher and student success and have made significant contributions toward innovative, unique, and effective career and technical education programs. The Administrator of the Year Award is sponsored by Goodheart-Willcox.

Dr. Donna Prudhomme serves as the Director of Career and Technical Education (CTE) for Beaumont Independent School District, bringing more than three decades of experience to her role, including 28 years within BISD and three in industry. She began her career teaching Criminal Justice and went on to serve as a high school counselor, assistant principal, magnet coordinator, and principal of Clifton J. Ozen Magnet High School. During her tenure as principal, the school earned state accountability ratings of Met Standard along with a state distinction in science.

A committed lifelong learner, Dr. Prudhomme holds five degrees from Lamar University, Prairie View A&M University, and Nova Southeastern University. She is certified as a Superintendent, Principal, School Counselor, and Vocational Trades and Industry teacher, reflecting her broad expertise in educational leadership.

Since stepping into the role of CTE Director in 2018, Dr. Prudhomme has led a transformation of BISD's CTE programs, focusing on rebranding efforts, program expansion, deeper community engagement, and the development of strong industry partnerships. One of her signature initiatives is the Annual CTE Choice Awards—an elaborate red-carpet celebration that now attracts more than 1,000 attendees each year to honor outstanding students, educators, and community partners.

Her leadership has driven significant gains in student achievement. Industry-based certification attainment has risen across the district, culminating in a major milestone in the 2024–2025 Accountability Ratings: BISD's CTE industry-based certification results for College, Career, and Military Readiness (CCMR) nearly match the State of Texas, with BISD at 34.9 percent and the state at 35 percent. BISD also surpasses the state average in Level I and Level II certificates, achieving 8.1 percent compared to the state's 1.1 percent.

Beyond her work in education, Dr. Prudhomme is a REALTOR®, a Board-Certified Credit Consultant, and the founder of the Credit Education School, a nonprofit organization dedicated to empowering young women through financial literacy. Her accomplishments have earned widespread recognition, including being named the 2024 CTAT

Administrator of the Year and the 2025 ACTE Region IV Administrator of the Year. She remains deeply committed to preparing students for success in college, career, and life.

Prudhomme was one of five finalists for the 2026 national title. The national winner was announced at the Awards Gala, recognizing the best CTE educators in the country. The event took place on December 9, at ACTE's CareerTech VISION 2025. The Awards Gala was sponsored by Express Employment Professionals, Goodheart-Willcox, The U.S. Army, and Stratasys.

The story was always enough. It just needed the right audience to finally hear it.

I share this not to list credentials but because of what that progression taught me. I thought I hadn't impressed the panel. I thought my story wasn't enough. But the story was always enough—it just needed the right audience and the right moment to be fully seen. That's exactly what this book is asking you to believe about Career and Technical Education. The programs have always been strong. The students have always been capable. The work has always been worthy. It simply needs leaders willing to tell the story with enough conviction that the right people in the right rooms will finally hear it.

We aren't alone in this work. And we never were.

The data was beginning to confirm what I'd been feeling for years. Recent national surveys showed that in 2025, 35 precent of parents said CTE was the best pathway for high-achieving students—up from just 13 percent in 2019. [5]

---

5 American Student Assistance, "New Survey Reveals Parents' Views on Their Children's Career Paths After High School," PR Newswire, 2025.

According to an American Staffing Association Workforce Monitor® survey conducted by The Harris Poll, a majority of US voters report highly favorable views of career and technical education—outpacing perceptions of traditional four-year colleges.[6]

The public was getting the message. The question I kept asking was, Why hadn't our schools gotten it yet?

After I was named the 2026 ACTE National Administrator of the Year, my lead BISDTV teacher, Kelvin Cormier, came to me wanting to create a video about my life story—*It's More Than Just an Elective: The Dr. Donna Prudhomme Story*. He had watched this journey unfold from behind the camera, filming our events, training our students, and telling the CTE story through his lens for years. When I shared with him that I had also been asked to deliver the keynote speech at the 2026 Summer K-12 CTE Congress Conference in Indianapolis, Indiana, he grinned from ear to ear. And then he shook his head and said something that stopped me in my tracks: "How is it that other people recognize our story, but we don't?"

I didn't have a clean answer for him in that moment. But I didn't need one. Because that question, asked by someone who had walked the same halls of this district as a student before returning to serve it as an educator, said everything this book is trying to say. Recognition doesn't always start at home. Sometimes the outside world sees your value before the people closest to you do. That isn't a reason to stop. That's a reason to keep telling the story—loudly, consistently, and without waiting for permission.

The recognition continued to come from places I didn't expect. I received a message from a freelance reporter for *EdTech: Focus on K–12* magazine—a

---

6 American Staffing Association, ASA Workforce Monitor® Survey, conducted by The Harris Poll, United States, October 27–31, 2022.

national publication reaching IT administrators, CTOs, and educational technologists across the K-12 setting. They wanted to schedule an interview to discuss being named Administrator of the Year, explore our work preparing students with workforce skills and job readiness, and learn how we ensure our district's offerings match local workforce needs and the specific initiatives at Beaumont ISD we're most proud of. Their photo editor reached out separately. They wanted to set up a photo shoot to accompany the story for their Spring 2026 print edition. A national magazine. A photo shoot. For CTE work happening in Beaumont, Texas. I thought about Kelvin's question: How is it that other people recognize our story but our own district doesn't? This was the answer. When you tell your story consistently and unapologetically, the right audience eventually finds it. And sometimes that audience is national.

But the recognition that stopped me completely didn't come from a magazine or a conference. It came in an envelope. My fourth-grade teacher, Kathie Duty, sent me a card with a *Beaumont Enterprise* newspaper clipping about my ACTE National Administrator of the Year award tucked inside. She wrote, "Congratulations on your latest of many achievements! I am so proud of you, as you are nationally recognized for outstanding leadership. What a deserving honor! It's obvious you are the same smart, sweet girl you exemplified in the fourth grade." Her penmanship was perfect. Just like I remembered seeing on the chalkboard. I sat with that for a long time. A woman who taught me when I was eight years old had watched from a distance long enough to see something in me that I hadn't yet seen in myself. And she took the time to write it down and send it. That's the kind of moment that reminds you that the people who planted seeds in you are still watching you grow.

Lamar University sent a card recognizing the award and affirming that my determination, passion, and talent had always made this moment possible. The institution that gave me my foundation was now witnessing what that foundation had built. And the Jefferson County Commissioners Office sent a congratulatory letter. The elected officials of the county I call home took the time to acknowledge what had been accomplished here. The community that raised me—my fourth-grade classroom, my university, my county—all looked up and said, "We see you. We always did."

Beaumont, Texas produced this. And Beaumont, Texas claimed it.

That realization was my turning point. It changed how I understood the problem—and therefore how I understood the solution. Until that moment, I'd been working within the system trying to improve programs, increase access, and provide more information. I believed that if we built strong enough programs, students would choose them. But that wasn't happening. And now I understood why. We were addressing the surface, not the root. The problem wasn't what we were offering. The problem was how it was being seen.

That realization shifted everything. I began to see that perception wasn't something that sat on the outside of the work. It was at the center of it. Instead of asking how to improve CTE, I started asking how to change how people experienced it. How do students see it? How do parents understand it? How do educators talk about it? Because experience shapes perception, and perception shapes decisions.

As we became more intentional, the results followed. Across every measure of student readiness, Beaumont ISD was performing at or above the state level. Advisory council members began speaking on our behalf, adding industry credibility to our narrative. Other districts started reaching out to learn from our approach. The city of Beaumont issued two proclamations recognizing Career and Technical Education, and the mayor of Beaumont attended our Principal Pop-In at the CTE Center. These weren't just programmatic milestones; they were signals that the narrative was beginning to shift beyond our schools and into the broader community.

But the most important shift was internal. I no longer saw perception as something separate from the work. I saw it as the work itself. Success was no longer just about program growth or participation numbers. It was about alignment—alignment between what we were offering and how it was being understood, between what we were saying and what students were experiencing, between perception and reality. When perception is aligned with reality, everything changes. That's when students choose with confidence. That's when parents support without hesitation. That's when educators lead with clarity. And that's when Career and Technical Education becomes what it has always had the potential to be.

PART

04

SHIFTING THE NARRATIVE

P — Prioritize Access and Equity |

T — Train the Influencers

CHAPTER 10

VISIBILITY BEFORE VIABILITY

You can't grow what people don't see

One of the most common assumptions in education is that strong programs will naturally attract participation. If the curriculum is rigorous, if the outcomes are clear, and if the opportunities are meaningful, students will come. But in practice, that's not what happens. Programs that are strong aren't always chosen. The missing piece is almost always the same: visibility.

You can't grow what people don't see. And even more importantly, you can't expect people to value what they don't fully understand. When I stepped into my role as director of CTE, one of the first things I recognized was that many of our programs were strong, but they weren't visible in a way that matched their value. Students didn't fully understand what was available to them. Parents were unfamiliar with the opportunities. Even staff members—including upper central office administration—didn't always have a clear picture of what CTE truly offered. The programs existed, but they weren't seen. And if they weren't seen, they couldn't be chosen.

> ***Visibility isn't marketing. It's the act of helping people see what is already true.***

I knew we needed to be different. To stand out. The inspiration came from an unexpected place— *Texas Country Reporter*, the longest-running independently produced television show in United States history. Created and hosted by Bob Phillips and his wife Kelli until September 2024, the show has traveled Texas since 1972, documenting uplifting stories of ordinary people and unique locations. Watching Bob Phillips bring the story to the people—going to where the community was rather than waiting for the community to come to him—sparked something in me. That's exactly what we needed to do with CTE.

So, through our K–8 Career Readiness initiative, we brought CTE directly to students rather than waiting for them to come to us. We put our assets on the road. We brought equipment, demonstrations, and real experiences to elementary and middle school campuses. Students were able to engage, explore, and experience what these pathways looked like in real time—not through a flyer or a career fair table but through hands-on interaction. When I say we brought it to them, I mean they were touching welding equipment, engaging with culinary setups, working with cosmetology hair models, driving a forklift simulator, using a venipuncture practice arm, and working with technology: real programs, real tools, real glimpses of real futures. That kind of visibility creates a different level of understanding. It moves CTE from something abstract to something real. And when something becomes real, it becomes possible.

The CTE Center is organized into nine academies—Agriculture; Architecture and Construction; Arts, Audio/Video Technology and Communications; Health Science; Hospitality and Tourism; Human Services, Law and Public Service; Manufacturing; Science Technology Engineering and Mathematics (STEM); and Transportation—each with its own dedicated program of study, industry-based certification pathway, and connection to the workforce of Southeast Texas. Students don't just take courses at the CTE Center. They enter an academy. And academies communicate something that a course list never could: that this is a place with identity, structure, and a clear destination.

February is nationally recognized as CTE Month. But don't wait until then to tell your story, and don't let that month pass without filling it completely. The most powerful CTE Month celebrations don't happen in isolation. They happen when you partner with the community so that CTE activities and events are woven throughout the entire month—in schools, in government chambers, and in community spaces where people already gather.

We made that happen intentionally. We partnered with Workforce Solutions Southeast Texas for the Youth Career Expo, an annual event held in February that introduces area high school youth to exciting career choices and pathways. We participated in Salute to Southeast Texas Workforce Month, a regional recognition of the workforce pipeline that connects education to industry across Southeast Texas. And we were honored at the Jefferson County Commissioner Meeting with a Salute to Southeast Texas Workforce Week Proclamation, a formal recognition from our county government that Career and Technical Education isn't just a school initiative. It's a community investment.

That recognition clarified something I had already begun to understand: If we aren't telling our story, it won't be told. So, we made a deliberate decision to celebrate CTE Month intentionally every February—highlighting students, showcasing programs, and creating opportunities for our community to see what had always been there. Throughout the month, we also dedicated time to CTSO Week, where students learn more about our career and technical student organizations: FFA, FCCLA, DECA, HOSA, TSA, and SkillsUSA.

When you partner with your community for CTE Month, you aren't just promoting a program. You're building a coalition. And coalitions change perception in ways that a single school event never can.

This is also a moment to showcase what our competitive CTE teams have been accomplishing. Future Farmers of America (FFA) wins local, district, and state competitions every year. Our FFA students aren't just learning about agriculture. They're competing at the highest levels, bringing home championships, and representing Beaumont ISD on stages that most people associate only with athletics. In areas from livestock judging to floriculture, from agricultural mechanics to public speaking, our FFA students are proving year after year that Career and Technical Education produces champions. In recent competition seasons, our FFA students earned Reserve Champion at the Houston Livestock Show and Rodeo (HLSR) Floral Design Texas Table Competition, claimed multiple championships and reserve championships at the Young Men's Business League (YMBL) South Texas State Fair, and generated over $54,000 in prize money through Livestock Supervised Agricultural Experience (SAE) projects. Under the leadership of Stephanie Hoppe, FFA has become one of the most decorated programs in our district.

Family, Career and Community Leaders of America (FCCLA) has won at the state competition for the past eight years, competing year-round and winning at the local and state level consistently. These aren't occasional wins. They're a standard of excellence that our FCCLA students have set and maintained season after season. For eight consecutive years, FCCLA students have competed annually at regional and state competitions in the event categories of Professional Presentation and Interpersonal Communications. Their success in areas like culinary arts, early childhood education, and family and consumer sciences reflects the rigor of our programs and the dedication of students who take their craft seriously enough to compete for it. Kelsey Jozwiak has built a program that doesn't just participate. It wins.

Distributive Education Clubs of America (DECA) has won state competitions for the past five years, and in 2026, our students made history by advancing to the international competition. In the most recent competition season, DECA produced thirty district qualifiers. Thirteen students advanced to state, and four students earned allocations to the International Career Development Conference in Orlando, standing alongside the best business and marketing students in the world. Our students earned that stage. They didn't stumble into it. They prepared for it, competed for it, and won their way there. That's not a footnote. That's a headline. Porsche Carr has created a culture of excellence in DECA that has made Beaumont ISD a name people know in competitive business education.

SkillsUSA students have been equally impressive. Our Cosmetology program students earned first place in the Customer Service Project at the district level. In HVAC—a program that connects directly to one of the highest-demand trades in Southeast Texas—two students placed at regionals, with one earning gold and advancing to state and one earning bronze. These are students competing in skilled trades at the highest levels of their field. That's not background noise. That's the headline that athletic championships share space with.

People need to know that athletic teams aren't the only teams winning state championships. I always remind Dr. Ron Jackson, our athletic director, that we win state championships in CTE, too. We toot our own horn. Not out of pride but out of responsibility.

Visibility also means creating opportunities outside of the traditional school calendar. We hosted a CTE Summer Exploration Camp for middle school students at the CTE Center and our agriculture farm. We opened those doors and invited students in to see, touch, and experience what CTE actually looked like—not through a brochure, not through a description, but in person. Summer isn't a break from the work of changing perception. It's an opportunity to reach students and families in a different context, with more time and less pressure. When students spend time at a career exploration camp, they aren't just learning about programs. They're experiencing them. They're trying things. They're discovering interests they didn't know they had. And they're returning to school in the fall with a different understanding of what CTE can offer them.

I stood in that space watching students walk through for the first time, and I wasn't prepared for what I heard. Again and again, students and the adults who brought them said some version of the same thing: "We didn't know you had all of this!" These were students from our own feeder schools. Future high school students who lived in this community. And they had no idea what was behind those doors or what was growing on that farm. That moment wasn't a celebration. It was a wake-up call. If our own middle school students didn't know what we had, we had a visibility problem. And visibility problems have solutions.

What began as a road show evolved into something even more intentional. The Middle School Career Launch Academy expanded Career and Technical Education directly into seventh and eighth grade—not just as exposure but as structured, credit-bearing coursework. Middle school students aren't simply visiting the CTE Center or watching a demonstration. They're earning high school credit while exploring career pathways. They're building toward a program of study before they ever set foot in a high school classroom. That's not just visibility. That's a head start. And when a student enters ninth grade already knowing what pathway they want to pursue, already having earned credit toward it, and already believing it's possible, the perception conversation changes entirely. We aren't convincing them to consider CTE. They're already in it.

The K–8 Career Readiness program isn't a single event. It's a comprehensive, age-appropriate system of activities and experiences designed to meet students where they are and grow with them as they develop. Our K–8 activities include the Future Ready Lab Tour, the CTE Road Show, the Career Exploration Summer Camp, job shadow opportunities, workplace tours, a student leadership conference, a soft skills program, and Xello—a career exploration platform introduced as early as kindergarten through second grade so that the youngest students in our district begin forming a relationship with the idea of careers before they can even fully read about them. In the 2024–2025 school year alone, 4,481 students participated in K–8 Career Readiness activities. That's not a footnote. That's a movement.

And then there's Build a Boat. Students design, build, and race boats—applying engineering principles, teamwork, and problem-solving in one of the most hands-on, joyful learning experiences we offer. It's the kind of activity that a student goes home and talks about at dinner. It's the kind of memory that surfaces years later when a high school student is choosing a pathway and something in them remembers, *I built something once. I was good at it. I want to do more of that.*

That's what a comprehensive K–8 visibility system does. It doesn't just inform students about CTE. It gives them experiences they carry with them—experiences that plant a seed long before the course selection conversation ever begins.

And then there are the electronic vehicle (EV) go-karts. In 2025, our Engineering Practicum teachers launched a class project where senior practicum students design and build EV go-karts at the CTE Center. These aren't remote-control toys. They're student-engineered electric vehicles—designed, assembled, and tested by seniors who have spent the year building toward exactly this kind of capstone experience. When a twelfth grader who started in Principles of Applied Engineering as a freshman crosses the finish line in a vehicle they built with their own hands, that isn't a class project. That's a career in motion. And when the students who haven't yet made it to senior year watch that happen, something shifts. Suddenly the pathway isn't abstract. It's visible. It's exciting. And it's worth four years of showing up.

Visibility also flows in the other direction. It isn't only about taking CTE out into the community; it's about bringing the community into CTE. We hold regular industry connection events where we invite industry partners directly into the CTE Center to connect with our students. These aren't career fairs with tables and brochures. They're real conversations between real professionals and students who are on the pathway to working alongside them. When a student in a health science program sits across from a hospital administrator, or when a construction student talks with a contractor who is hiring, something shifts. The pathway stops being theoretical. It becomes a relationship. And relationships build belief in ways that flyers or presentations never could. We also hold mock interviews in which industry professionals sit across from our students and put them through a realistic interview experience. Students practice how to present themselves, how to answer questions about their skills and certifications, and how to carry themselves as professionals. When a student walks out of a mock interview with feedback from someone who actually does the hiring, they leave with something no classroom lesson can fully replicate: confidence grounded in real experience. That's visibility at its deepest level—not just showing students what's possible but putting them inside the possibility so they can feel what it's like to belong there.

But perhaps the most powerful visibility moment we created wasn't for students or parents or community members. It was for the leaders inside our own system. In celebration of CTE Month 2024, we launched Day in the Life of a CTE Teacher, inviting district administrators and campus leaders to spend approximately two hours inside a designated CTE program as active participants in a hands-on simulation activity. Our superintendent spent two hours in Welding. Our executive director of curriculum and instruction suited up for Diesel and Heavy Equipment. One assistant superintendent experienced Collision and Repair. Another assistant superintendent worked in Carpentry. Our athletic director worked in Animal Science at the agriculture farm. Our senior director of student support services experienced Cosmetology. Our transportation director participated in Engineering. The executive director of human resources spent the morning in Floral Design. The chief financial officer reported for BISDTV. And our high school principals competed against each other in a Beaumont United vs. West Brook culinary cook-off, putting their skills and their school pride on the line in a CTE kitchen. The entire experience was filmed over two weeks by our BISDTV teachers and students, capturing district leaders discovering firsthand what CTE actually looks like from the inside. When a superintendent puts on a welding helmet and stands in front of a torch, when a high school principal ties on an apron and competes in a culinary cook-off—something changes. They can't unsee it. They can't un-feel it. And the next time a conversation happens in a cabinet meeting or a board room about what CTE is and why it matters, those leaders aren't speaking theoretically. They're speaking from experience. That's visibility doing its deepest work.

One of the largest visibility moments we've been part of was the BISD–ExxonMobil Family STEM Night at Ford Park in Beaumont, led by LaChandra Cobb-Eaglin, my coordinator of STEM. More than seven thousand families from across Southeast Texas came together to learn about engineering, science, technology, and the career pathways connected to those fields. ExxonMobil is one of the largest employers in our region, and their partnership with BISD created an event that went far beyond anything a school building could contain. Seven thousand families. In one place. Engaging with CTE and STEM pathways. That's visibility at a scale that changes the community's relationship with Career and Technical Education—not just for a day but in the conversations that happen at dinner tables for weeks afterward. You can't replicate that reach through a flyer or a school newsletter. You build it by putting CTE in spaces where the community is already gathering, alongside partners who already have their trust.

The ExxonMobil partnership didn't happen in isolation. It grew from a deliberate investment in STEM programming that we'd been building inside our district. Our STEM vision is simple and ambitious at the same time: "to foster the curiosity of students in the areas of Science, Technology, Engineering, and Mathematics (STEM) to help build a strong pipeline into our future workforce." What we offer reflects that vision: Principles of Engineering, Robotics I and II, Computer Science I and II, Engineering Design and Presentation, and Practicum in Engineering. These aren't elective diversions. They're rigorous, sequential pathways that connect directly to the industries driving the economy of Southeast Texas. When ExxonMobil shows up to a STEM event with seven thousand families, they aren't doing us a favor. They're investing in a pipeline they helped us build.

But the STEM work extends far beyond one event. Under LaChandra Cobb-Eaglin's leadership, our STEM programming reaches students at every level. We offer a Seventh Grade Bridge to STEM and a Summer Bridge to STEM to ensure students are building their STEM foundation before they ever set foot in a high school engineering classroom. We sponsor elementary STEM clubs so that curiosity is nurtured long before it becomes a course selection. We provide STEM resources for middle school classes and instructional materials for high school engineering and robotics courses. We support students participating in robotics competitions and organize STEM field trips that take learning beyond the classroom walls. In the 2024–2025 school year, 523 students were enrolled in the high school STEM pathway, and 600 students were enrolled in middle school STEM courses. This isn't a single program. It's a pipeline built deliberately, sustained intentionally, and designed to ensure that every student in Beaumont ISD has a pathway into the future of work.

At the center of our work-based learning strategy is what we call the R.E.A.L. Program—Real Experience and Learning. Our motto is "Work-Based Learning is where it gets REAL." It's where the classroom meets the career, where the certification meets the employer, and where the student meets the version of themselves they've been working toward. My coordinator of business and industry, Eva LeBlanc, manages our business and industry partnerships—attending meetings, building relationships, and ensuring that CTE is always in the loop on workforce needs and employment opportunities.

Because of that work, our students aren't just learning about careers. They're connected to the people who are hiring for them.

The R.E.A.L. Program operates through two primary purposes. The first is Career Preparation and Practicum: structured internship experiences that place students in real work environments alongside real employers. Our health science students complete pre-practicum hospital rotations, working alongside healthcare professionals in actual clinical settings before they ever graduate. These aren't field trips. They're supervised, professional experiences that prepare students for immediate entry into the workforce.

The second purpose is our CTE student enterprises: real businesses operated by real students, generating real revenue within their programs of study. The Ag Farm Floral Shop operates on our agriculture farm. IndustrialED Solutions serves the Architecture and Construction program. As mentioned, BISDTV is a fully functioning television production enterprise run by our Audio Visual Technology students—the same students who livestream our football games and produce content for our CTE YouTube channel. Designergy operates within our Graphic Design program. Southern Comfort Catering operates out of our Culinary Arts program. The Glamour Shop is run by our Cosmetology students. And Auto Repair R US is operated by our Transportation and Logistics students.

These aren't simulated businesses in the theoretical sense. They're functioning enterprises where students apply their skills, serve real customers, and generate revenue for their programs. That's not a classroom exercise. That's a career in progress.

Consistency is equally critical. It isn't enough to highlight CTE once or twice a year. It must be part of the ongoing conversation, showing up in multiple spaces and multiple forms over time. Because perception isn't built in a single moment; it's built through repeated exposure to the same message, told in different ways, until it begins to feel familiar and true.

As we continued this work, the shift became measurable. Students were asking more questions. Parents were becoming more engaged. Staff were speaking about CTE with greater confidence and specificity.

Visibility must come before viability. You can have the strongest program in the world, but if it isn't visible, it won't reach its full potential.

CHAPTER 11

BRANDING CTE LIKE IT MATTERS

Identity, presence, and positioning

Branding is often misunderstood in education. When leaders hear the word, they sometimes think of logos, taglines, and marketing campaigns—surface-level tools that belong in the business world, not in schools. But branding, at its core, is about identity. It's about ensuring that what you stand for is consistently communicated and consistently understood. I always tell my team that we have to protect our brand—put our logo on everything we produce, stay in our brand colors, and ensure that whatever we put out represents the best of who we are. Because when people see your brand, they aren't just seeing a logo. They're seeing a standard. And that standard has to be worth protecting. In that sense, branding isn't separate from the work of leadership. It's an extension of it.

For Career and Technical Education, branding is not optional. Without a clear and consistent identity, CTE is left to be defined by whoever is in the room—and that person may be working from assumptions, outdated perceptions, or incomplete information. Branding gives CTE the ability to define itself before someone else does. That isn't marketing. That's leadership.

When I began focusing on perception, one of the first practical shifts I made was around how CTE showed up visually and verbally across our district. We had already built the foundation—a logo, colors, messaging, blazers for staff and student representatives, a professional photo and video shoot that said we take this work seriously. Those tools created a recognizable identity that other departments began to replicate. That replication told me something important: When a brand is built with clarity and conviction, people notice. And when they notice, culture begins to shift.

We also created a theme—*Find Your Future*—which became the name of our CTE magazine, a publication produced by our department that tells our story in our own words. Every program. Every pathway. Every opportunity. Every student. *Find Your Future* isn't just a slogan. It's a promise to every student who opens that magazine and sees themselves in its pages, to every parent who reads it and begins to understand what CTE actually offers, and to every community member who holds it and realizes for the first time that Career and Technical Education isn't what they thought it was. A publication that tells your story is a visibility tool that keeps working long after the event is over, the post has scrolled past, and the announcement has been forgotten. It lives on a kitchen table. It sits in a waiting room. It gets passed from one parent to another. *Find Your Future* was designed to go wherever our students and families went—and to keep telling the story when we weren't in the room to tell it ourselves.

> ***When CTE is branded like it matters, people start to believe that it does.***

We also made structural branding decisions that went beyond visuals. We decided that IBC teachers deserved the same public recognition as any other educator producing results for students. So we gave them that recognition on our own stage. At the CTE Choice Awards, IBC teachers walked the red carpet

Grammy-style—complete with a hype walk-up song played by the DJ—to receive their Best Teacher Performance award in front of their peers, their students, and their community.

Structure communicates value more powerfully than any memo or mission statement ever could. When you put someone on the same stage as what's already celebrated, you're making a statement about what deserves to be celebrated. That was a branding decision. And it changed how CTE teachers saw themselves—and how everyone in that room saw them.

The CTE Choice Awards represented the fullest expression of our branding work. But before I tell you what we built, I want to tell you what we're working against—and what we're working toward.

In 2026, both of our high school boys basketball teams made history and went to the 5A UIL State Championship at the Alamodome in San Antonio, Texas. Families and community members made the four-hour, 279-mile drive from Beaumont without a second thought. It was a packed house. Energy filled every seat of one of the largest arenas in the country. Nobody had to be convinced to attend. Nobody needed a special incentive. Nobody required a particular venue or a carefully designed experience to walk through those doors. People showed up because the culture had already decided that those students and that achievement were worth showing up for.

That's the standard I had in mind when we built the CTE Choice Awards. Not competition with athletics. There's no us versus them in this work. Our student athletes and our CTE students are often the same students. The goal was never to compete. The goal was to close the gap in how achievement is perceived and celebrated across different areas of student excellence. When you don't have to pull out the red carpet for people to attend, it means the culture already values what's happening inside. We weren't there yet with CTE. So, we pulled out the red carpet—deliberately, unapologetically, and with intention.

The CTE Choice Awards became exactly what we intended it to be—not just an annual event but a cultural statement. By the time our superintendent, cabinet members, and school board members were sitting front and center every single year, something had shifted. What began as a deliberate act of visibility had become an expectation. A tradition. A standard. Our students weren't just attending a recognition ceremony. They were walking into their championship event. Their CTE graduation. And they knew it before they ever walked through the door.

That's what intentional narrative change looks like in practice. You don't wait for the culture to value something before you celebrate it. You celebrate it at the level it deserves, consistently and visibly, until the culture catches up.

The CTE Choice Awards wasn't an event. It was a statement. And families came. There were lines out the door of the Beaumont Civic Center. The food served that evening was prepared by our culinary students. The venue was draped with beautiful floral arrangements designed and created by our floral design students. Our BISDTV students livestreamed and videoed the entire event, capturing every moment, every award, every student walking across that stage. It wasn't a school event with CTE students in attendance. It was a CTE student-run event, from the kitchen to the stage to the camera. Every element of the evening was a demonstration of what our students could do. Students were recognized in spaces and ways they had never experienced before. Other districts began calling to ask how we had done it and what they could borrow. That's when you know branding is working: when it inspires replication.

To extend the brand beyond our team and into the student community, we created CTE Ambassadors. Select students from both high schools were trained to be the student voices of CTE—representing their programs, sharing their experiences, and telling the CTE story in their own words to peers, parents, and community members. This was a deliberate decision rooted in a simple truth: No one communicates the value of CTE more credibly than a student who has lived it. Adults can describe what a program offers, but students can describe what it feels like. And feeling is what changes minds. Our CTE Ambassadors became walking proof that CTE isn't a fallback option. It's a first choice. It's an identity. It's something worth representing with pride.

Positioning is the final piece. Branding defines identity, but positioning determines how that identity is understood in relation to everything else. We began to intentionally frame CTE as complementary to college, not in competition with it. A student could pursue CTE and college. A student could earn a certification and a degree. CTE was not a ceiling; it was a launch pad. When CTE is branded like it matters and positioned as a first-class pathway, people start to believe that it is. And when they believe it, they choose it.

CHAPTER 12

REMOVING BARRIERS TO ACCESS

Scheduling, pathways, and equity

Access is often described in simple terms—whether a program exists, whether a course is offered, whether a student has the opportunity to enroll. On paper, access can appear straightforward: A program is available, seats are open, and students are allowed to sign up. But in practice, access is far more complex. True access isn't just about availability. It's about whether students can engage in an opportunity without unnecessary barriers. And whether the system is designed in a way that allows students to pursue what aligns with their interests and goals without being forced into trade-offs that quietly communicate which pathways matter more.

> ***Access must be real, not theoretical. A door that's hard to open is effectively closed.***

The sequencing of CTE pathways should be as straightforward as any core subject in the building. English I, English II, English III, English IV—four years, four levels, one clear progression from ninth grade through twelfth. Nobody questions that sequence. Nobody asks whether a student is ready for English II before they've completed English I. The pathway is understood, respected, and protected in every master schedule in every high school in the country.

CTE pathways work the same way—sequentially. Level I through Level IV. Ninth grade through twelfth grade. While graduation requirements vary by state, CTE is commonly categorized as electives rather than required subject areas. A student can fulfill their elective requirements without a single CTE course and still walk across that graduation stage. And that distinction, however structural it may sound, communicates something to every principal, every counselor, and every scheduler who builds a master schedule: When something has to give, CTE gives first.

In Texas, the Texas Education Agency defines a CTE Completer as a student who completes, passes, and receives credit for three or more high school CTE courses within the same program of study, totaling at least four credits and including at least one advanced course at Level 3 or Level 4. While the specific requirements vary by state, the principle is the same everywhere: CTE completion requires a multi-year sequence of intentional planning, consistent enrollment, and a master schedule that protects the pathway from the first year to the last. When scheduling treats CTE as an elective to be filled in around everything else, Completers become impossible. And when Completers become impossible, credentials become out of reach.

But here's what that framing misses. A student can graduate without being a CTE Completer. But can they compete without it? Graduation is the floor. Career readiness is the ceiling. And CTE is one of the most direct routes from one to the other. Break the sequence, and you break the pipeline. Protect the sequence, and you protect the student.

Equity is another critical dimension that can't be separated from this conversation. True access means that all students—regardless of background, academic level, or prior experience—have the opportunity to explore and engage in Career and Technical Education. For too long, CTE has been associated with certain groups of students, and that association has limited who feels invited to participate. I saw this clearly during my time as a high school counselor, when the persistent belief that only special education students attended the CTE Center shaped who considered those programs and who didn't. That belief wasn't based on reality. But it shaped behavior, and behavior shapes outcomes.

The CCMR framework is also one of the most powerful tools we have for removing the perception barrier around CTE. When students and parents understand that achieving an industry-based certification or a Level I certificate earns a CCMR point, the conversation changes. CTE isn't a separate track. It's a recognized, state-validated pathway to graduation readiness. Students who complete CTE programs and earn their CCMR point can also wear copper cords at graduation: a visible, public signal that their achievement belongs on the same stage as every other form of student success. Our CCMR coordinators, Olivia Douglas at Beaumont United High School and Sadie Ambrose at West Brook High School (who replaced Jennifer Chambers-Moore, who was promoted to director of CTE at another district in 2025) carry this message to students and families every day. Olivia is a former student of mine from Ozen High School, and watching her now guide students toward the same kinds of opportunities she once navigated is exactly what the alumni hiring philosophy looks like in practice. The system is designed to reward CTE achievement. Our job is to make sure every student, parent, and counselor knows it.

When high-achieving students are visible in CTE programs, when their presence normalizes the pathway, it sends a message to every other student that there's no ceiling on who belongs here. Our valedictorians and salutatorians, Division I athletes, basketball state champions, cheerleaders, and drill team members have been enrolled in pathways like Culinary Arts, Health Science, Engineering, and

Welding at the CTE Center. CTE is not a consolation path. It's the path that our highest achievers are choosing alongside their academic coursework. This is why representation inside the programs matters as much as access to them. Removing barriers requires challenging those perceptions and ensuring that CTE is positioned and experienced as a pathway for all students.

Logistical barriers also matter more than leaders often acknowledge. Transportation to internships, location, and program placement all influence whether students are able to participate. When programs are moved to different campuses—even when the move is made for sound programmatic reasons—the change in location can create a barrier that not every student has the resources to navigate. I saw this in my own son's story. When the program he needed was moved to another campus, a barrier was introduced that would have caused many students to redirect. He stayed the course. But we can't build a system that depends on students having the determination to push past structural obstacles we created.

The design of CTE pathways as intentional, sequential programs of study, organized into four levels aligned to grade progression—Level I through Level IV—communicates something critical to students, parents, and counselors: CTE is not a class you take. It's is a pathway you build.

Level IV courses are practicum classes—the capstone of the pathway where students move beyond the classroom and into real-world application. Our seniors are placed in internships on campus, within the district, or off campus in the community, depending on their program and goals. They're working alongside industry professionals, applying the skills they've been building for three years, and experiencing what their future career field actually looks and feels like before they graduate. That isn't a field trip. That's career preparation in its truest form.

Career Preparation and Practicum opportunities are designed to introduce senior students to real work environments and provide training for entry-level positions in the workforce. The practicum gives students supervised, practical application of the knowledge and skills they've been building since Level 1. Internships are embedded within practicum courses. And a variety of our programs of study culminate with an internship placement—on campus, within the district, or off campus in the community—so that every student who completes a CTE pathway has real-world experience before they graduate. Work-based learning is not an add-on to the program. It's the point of the program. And when students graduate with not just a certification but a practicum experience and a professional reference from an actual employer, the barrier between education and employment begins to disappear.

The R.E.A.L. (Real Experience and Learning) Program didn't arrive fully formed. It was built slowly, deliberately, and against real resistance.

Prior to 2020, business and industry partnerships were predominantly assigned district partners connected to the CTE campus. The relationships existed on paper more than in practice. When we launched in the 2020–2021 school year, we had no internships and no training stations. We were virtual. The entire concept of connecting students to real work environments felt distant when students couldn't even be in the building. But we began building the framework anyway because we knew that when the doors opened, we needed to be ready.

In 2021–2022, the doors opened. But business and industry were hesitant. COVID-19 had changed everything. Employers were cautious about bringing students into their workplaces. And our district carried a perceived reputation in the community that made the sell even harder. We were asking industry partners to trust us with their time, their facilities, and their professional environments. And many of them were not yet sure we'd earned that trust.

In 2022–2023, something began to shift. Business and industry partners started to believe in what we were doing. They saw the students. They saw the certifications. They saw the seriousness of the programs and the professionalism of the young people coming through our doors. The hesitation began to give way to investment.

From 2023 to present, we've experienced consistent growth in business and industry partnerships, and that growth has been the direct result of relationships built on proof. Not promises. Proof. Every student who showed up prepared, every certification that was earned, every employer who hired from our programs became the evidence that CTE in Beaumont ISD was worth partnering with.

Our work-based learning continuum spans every stage of a student's educational journey: career awareness beginning in pre-K and elementary, career exploration in middle school, career preparation in high school, and career training at the post-secondary level. This isn't a high school program with a catchy name. It's a deliberate, sequential system that begins before students can drive and doesn't stop until they're employed.

The scale of that work-based learning commitment is significant. In the 2024–2025 school year, 128 high school students participated in internships, business and industry employment, and observational rotations—real placements with real employers in real career fields. Another 2,182 students gained experience through CTE labs and simulated work environments: forty-two labs across our district designed to replicate the tools, equipment, and expectations of actual industry settings. And seventy-four students participated in mentorship and leadership programs: one-on-one connections with professionals who invested their time in the next generation of the workforce. As mentioned earlier, we also operate seven CTE student enterprises—real businesses run by real students generating real revenue. These aren't hypothetical numbers. They're the evidence of a work-based learning system that's functioning at scale and producing results.

Our juniors and seniors in advanced Level III and Level IV courses are bused to the CTE Center to access programs that require specialized labs, equipment, and instructional environments that can't be replicated on a home campus. At the same time, we recognize that transportation can itself become a barrier—which is why some of our programs of study allow students to remain on their home campus through what we call a home campus completion pathway. This gives students the opportunity to complete their CTE sequence in a setting that removes the logistical challenge of cross-campus travel while still accessing a rigorous, industry-aligned program. The goal in every case is the same: Ensure that the structure of the pathway serves the student, not the other way around.

As we addressed these barriers, the impact was clear. Students who had previously been unable to access certain programs began to engage. Participation increased not because we added more programs but because we made existing programs more accessible. That's the power of removing barriers. It doesn't require starting from scratch. It requires rethinking what already exists with equity and access as the guiding principles.

CHAPTER 13

TRAINING THE INFLUENCERS

Counselors, teachers, and leaders must believe first

Students don't make decisions alone. They make them in conversation with teachers who notice their strengths, with counselors who help them choose courses, with administrators who shape what's available, and with peers who reflect what's respected. These adults aren't just participants in the system. They're influencers within it. If we want to change what students choose, we have to change what the influencers believe. That's where the real work begins.

For years, I saw strong programs struggle to gain traction, not because they lacked value but because the people guiding students didn't fully understand or believe in that value. Even when educators supported Career and Technical Education in theory, their confidence in communicating it wasn't always consistent or compelling. Students can feel that. They can sense hesitation. They can hear the difference between a recommendation that's confident and one that's cautious. That difference matters because students aren't just listening to what's said. They're interpreting how it's said.

> ***Training influencers isn't about giving them information. It's about changing what they believe.***

I was a high school counselor from 2002 to 2008, and I'll always have a sweet spot in my heart for counselors. I've always felt that counselors are the heartbeat of the campus. They're at the core of how a school functions, how students are guided, and how futures are shaped one conversation at a time. But one thing I noticed then and still notice now is that counselors are underpaid, overworked, and always get the blame. They're blamed when students aren't in the correct pathway. They're blamed when students are removed from the CTE Center. They're blamed when students get scheduled into athletics before CTE. But many of them are simply taking orders—from principals, from parents, and from systems that don't always align with what's best for students. It's an impossible position, and most counselors are in it because they genuinely care.

I often have this conversation with our director of guidance and counseling, Lydia Sylvester, who has a heart of gold but frequently finds herself and her counselors caught in the middle, navigating competing priorities while trying to do what's right for every student who walks through their door. The problem is rarely the counselor. The problem is the system the counselor is operating inside of. And when we talk about training influencers, we have to start by acknowledging that some of our most important influencers are working under conditions that make it very difficult to advocate for the right pathway every time. Changing what counselors believe is only half the work. The other half is changing the systems that constrain what they're able to do with that belief.

Training influencers also means bringing educators into CTE spaces physically. As I've shared, we brought teachers and counselors into our programs, allowed them to see students engaged in real technical work, and connected them with industry partners who could speak directly to workforce needs and earning potential. We made it engaging and fun. Our CTE teachers participated in a scavenger hunt to learn more about the CTE Center, discovering programs, spaces, and opportunities they'd never fully explored.

We also used Kahoot! games during professional development to teach CTE history. Because when educators know the story of where CTE came from and what it has become, they tell that story differently to students.

Learning doesn't have to be passive to be powerful. When educators see the real-world impact with their own eyes, and when they experience it in ways that are interactive and memorable, their perspective shifts in a way that no handout or presentation can achieve.

We also leveraged our advisory council members as part of this process. Our twenty-three-member CTE Advisory Council includes representatives from ExxonMobil, Acadian Ambulance, Baptist Hospitals of SETX, CHRISTUS Southeast Texas Health System, Associated Builders and Contractors Southeast Texas, Lamar Institute of Technology, Lamar University College of Engineering, the Greater Beaumont Chamber of Commerce, the Jefferson County Sheriff's Office, the Port of Beaumont, and Workforce Solutions SETX, among others, representing over one hundred business and industry partners involved in various CTE programs and initiatives across our district. These aren't honorary appointments. These are the people who hire our students. When they stood up and vouched for what we were doing, it added a layer of credibility that changed conversations at every level, connecting CTE to real careers, real salaries, and real opportunities in ways our own advocacy sometimes couldn't.

A partnership only works when both parties bring something the other genuinely needs and when the collaboration makes both stronger than they were separately. For CTE, that means industry partners aren't just donors or guest speakers. They're invested stakeholders who bring workforce credibility, real-world context, and hiring power to the table. And in return, CTE brings them something equally valuable: a trained, certified, career-ready pipeline of young people who already understand their industry before they ever walk through the door. That's not charity. That's a mutual investment. And when both sides understand what they're bringing and what they're gaining, the partnership becomes something neither could have built alone.

This is why our advisory council members don't just attend meetings. They show up at our events. They speak to our students. They post on their own platforms about what they've witnessed inside our programs. They recruit from our classrooms. They donate to our students. They do these things not because we asked them to but because the partnership gave them something worth protecting. When an industry partner believes in what you're building, they don't wait to be invited. They find their own way in. And that's when you know the partnership is real.

We also had to shift how educators saw themselves. When I told CTE teachers, "You're just as important as core teachers. The state holds us accountable for 40 percent, just like them," it wasn't about defending our accountability metrics. It's not us versus them—core versus CTE. We're all on the same team, working toward the same goal: student success. It was about professional identity and worth. Because when educators see themselves as important, they communicate that importance to students through every interaction. And when counselors present a CTE pathway with the same confidence and enthusiasm they bring to a college preparatory course, students receive a fundamentally different message about what that pathway means and where it can lead.

Operation IBC wasn't a reaction. It was a proactive strategic initiative built like a military operation because that's exactly what it required. The name was intentional. IBC attainment was our mission. And just like any military operation, it required a clear objective, a detailed plan, assigned roles, and a commitment to leaving no one behind.

Each campus had an individualized IBC Strategic Action Plan—one for Beaumont United High School, one for West Brook High School, and one for the Career and Technical Education Center. This wasn't a one-size-fits-all approach. Each plan was built around the specific programs, students, and certification exams on that campus. Because what a cosmetology student needs to pass her licensing exam is different from what a welding student needs to pass his NCCER certification. And our plans reflected that.

At its core, Operation IBC was a teacher training and support initiative. We started with the teachers because that's where every student outcome begins. Teachers received firsthand experience with the IBC exams themselves—not just curriculum training but actual exposure to the assessments their students would face. You can't fully prepare someone for something you have never experienced yourself. We made sure our teachers had experienced it. From there, we built the infrastructure around them: curriculum timelines, practice testing protocols with a target score of 800 required to advance to the next training level, in-class study sessions, online teacher training modules, and a shared Google Drive folder—the Operation IBC resource hub—where every tool, every plan, and every data point lived in one place accessible to the entire team.

We also built a Professional Learning Community (PLC) structure we called Team Up Wednesday—meeting the first Wednesday of every month to discuss assessment data together. Teachers pulled their own data reports. They reviewed quizzes and test scores. They identified students in need of remediation. They planned re-teaching when the data required it. This wasn't a top-down accountability meeting. It was a collaborative professional learning community where teachers owned their data and drove their own improvement. That distinction matters. Because teachers who own their data are more invested in their students' outcomes than teachers who simply receive feedback from above.

We set a passing goal of 90 percent. We tracked every student. And we built in incentives that connected IBC achievement to the things students already cared about: the dark green IBC cord worn at the CTE Choice Awards and carried across the graduation stage, the copper CCMR cord recognizing College, Career, and Military Readiness, morning and afternoon announcements celebrating newly certified students by name, an end-of-year celebration, and exemption from final exams for students who pass their IBC. That last one matters more than people realize. When a student knows that passing their industry certification exempts them from a final exam, the certification stops feeling like an extra burden. It becomes a reward. And when the reward is visible—when the cord is real and the recognition is public—students pursue it.

This wasn't casual. This was a system built before anyone required it. Because we already believed the work was worth doing at the highest level. Operation IBC sent a message to every teacher on every campus: We aren't going to hand you a certification requirement and walk away. We're going to build the system around you, give you the tools, sit in the data with you, and celebrate every student who crosses that finish line. That's what it looks like when a department believes its teachers are just as important as any other educator in the building.

But Operation IBC is only one part of how we support our teachers. The real work happens in the ongoing, sustained presence we maintain on every campus throughout the year.

We instituted CTE Walks—a dedicated day when our team conducts walkthroughs at each campus, individually and together. These aren't compliance visits. They're instructional support visits built around "grows and glows," recognizing what teachers are doing well and providing specific, actionable feedback to help them go further. We also bring signs of support—visible, tangible reminders that the CTE department is invested in every teacher's success. The goal is simple: No CTE teacher should ever feel like they are doing this work alone.

We also hold beginning-of-year, middle-of-year, and end-of-year CTE Table Talks—structured campus visits designed to ensure that all the moving parts are still aligned and moving toward our goals. At the beginning of the year, we set the direction together. At the middle of the year, we check the data, identify gaps, and adjust the plan. At the end of the year, we celebrate what was accomplished and documented what needs to carry forward. These aren't administrative check-ins. They're collaborative conversations that keep every campus connected to the same mission throughout the entire school year.

And every teacher in our department receives a CTE Instructional Binder: a comprehensive resource tool containing the curriculum frameworks, IBC pacing guides, instructional strategies, and program of study materials they need to deliver rigorous, aligned instruction. The binder isn't just a document. It's a signal. It says, "You're a professional, your work is structured and supported, and this department has done the work to give you what you need before you ever have to ask for it."

Together these initiatives—Operation IBC, CTE Walks, Beginning, Middle, and End of Year Table Talks, and CTE Instructional Binders—form a complete instructional support system. Not episodic. Not reactive. Sustained, structured, and consistent from the first day of school to the last. That's what it looks like when a department truly believes its teachers are the most important influencers in the building.

Professional development wasn't a one-time event in our department. It's a calendar commitment. Every August, we hold CTE professional development to launch the school year: setting the instructional direction, reviewing program expectations, and ensuring every CTE teacher walks into their first day with clarity about what the year requires of them. Every October, we return: checking in on the work, adjusting strategies based on early data, and keeping the momentum from the first weeks of school from fading. And every

February during CTE Month, we hold professional development again: reconnecting teachers to the mission, celebrating early wins, and pushing toward the final stretch of the year with renewed focus. Three times a year. Every year. Consistently.

But the most powerful professional development doesn't always come from the front of the room. It comes from the person in the classroom next door. I made a deliberate decision to recognize CTE teachers who were excelling in their classrooms and elevate them as exemplars for their peers. These teachers don't just receive recognition. They become CTE Instructional Coaches, presenting during our professional development sessions and sharing the strategies, systems, and practices that were producing real results in their classrooms. This is intentional. When a teacher learns from another teacher who's doing the same work in the same context—not a consultant, not a central office administrator, but someone who teaches the same students in the same building—the learning lands differently. It's credible. It's practical. And it sends a message to every teacher in the room that excellence in this department is recognized, celebrated, and worth sharing.

We also participate in the Annual Elementary and Secondary Curriculum Conference, bringing our teachers and administrators together with educators from across the region to learn, grow, and stay connected to what's happening in education beyond our district. Because the best professional development doesn't just happen inside your own building. Sometimes it requires stepping outside of what's familiar and sitting in a room with people who challenge you to think differently about the work you're already doing.

Together these professional development touchpoints—August, October, and February sessions, CTE Instructional Coaches presenting from their own classrooms, and the Annual Curriculum Conference—create a sustained learning culture in our department. Not because we're required to but because we believe that teachers who keep growing produce students who keep growing. And in a department that's asking teachers to prepare students for careers that are constantly evolving, standing still is never an option.

We also connect our teachers to the professional development resources available through Region 5 Education Service Center. The Region 5 ESC team provides numerous workshops throughout the year—some specific to CTE content areas, and others focused on broader educational topics, including special education, pedagogy, and English learner support. Our teachers can search the Region 5 workshop catalog by title, date, category, and Texas Teacher Evaluation and Support System (T-TESS) domain, giving them access to a wide range of learning opportunities beyond what we provide internally. Because professional growth doesn't stop at the walls of our department. The best CTE teachers are always learning—from their colleagues, from their industry partners, from their regional service center, and from every space that challenges them to grow. We make sure those doors are open and that our teachers know how to walk through them.

One of the most intentional influencer strategies I pursued was hiring district graduates to serve as teachers. When I became principal at Ozen High School in 2016, one of my first goals was to hire as many alumni as possible—people who had once walked the breezeway at 3443 Fannett Road. I had at least fourteen staff members who were Ozen graduates. Edward Taylor Sr. returned as head football coach. Michael Thomas became head boys basketball coach. Shonte Leonard served as director of student activities. The most powerful influencers aren't always the ones we recruit or train from the outside. Sometimes they're the students we invested in who came back.

Olivia Douglas was my student when I served as a high school counselor at Ozen High School. I sat across from her, helped her think through her future, and tried to be the kind of counselor who left students better than I found them. At the time, she was a science teacher, but she was always moving. She went on to become an elementary counselor and then a CCMR coordinator, building a career in the exact space where student futures are shaped.

Years later, we stood on the same stage at the CTAT Excellence Awards—two educators from the same district, winning in the same year, making history together. Olivia was named the 2024 CTAT Guidance and Career Development Professional of the Year. The field I had once helped her navigate became the field she was celebrated for leading.

That's what intentional investment looks like when it comes full circle. We talk about training influencers as though they're always someone new, someone external, someone we have yet to reach. But sometimes the influencer you need is already in your building—sitting in a desk, waiting for someone to believe in them first.

And then there was Porsche Carr, who started as a permanent science substitute teacher and later became a CTE business teacher and CTE department head. She started DECA, and every year since, that program has advanced at state, national, and now international competitions. Keisha Kirkwood went from science teacher and department head to lead health science teacher at the CTE Center—taking the same passion for science she'd developed as a student and channeling it into preparing the next generation of health care professionals. Kelvin Cormier, Joshua Lamb, Galen Douglas, Diamonique Prudhomme, and Amanda Wood leading BISDTV—these are just a few of my former students who are leading and impacting our students in a phenomenal way.

Watching former students who once walked those hallways fill key positions and give back to their community is one of the greatest privileges of this work. These weren't just hiring decisions. They were investments in a community that already believed in itself. When alumni come back, they don't just bring their skills. They bring their love for the place that shaped them. And students feel that every single day.

When a student walks into a CTE classroom, and the teacher at the front is someone who graduated from their own high school or district—someone who sat in the same seats, walked the same halls, and built a career through the very pathways now being offered—the message is immediate and undeniable. You can do this. Not because someone told you so but because the person standing in front of you is living proof. Alumni who return as teachers don't just bring content knowledge. They bring credibility that no outside hire can replicate. They know the community. They know the culture. And students know them. That recognition changes the dynamic in the room from the very first day.

We have living proof of this in our own district. Our welding teachers are a sister and brother—both of whom went through our welding program as students. They sat in those same lab seats. They learned the same skills. And then they came back to teach the next generation of students in the same program that shaped them. I want to pause on that for a moment because the sister is particularly significant. Welding is historically a male-dominated field. Seeing a woman not only master the craft but return to teach it sends a powerful message to every young woman who walks into that lab: This space belongs to you, too. She isn't just a teacher. She's a statement. When a student in that welding lab looks at their teacher and knows that person was once exactly where they're sitting, the pathway stops being hypothetical. It becomes a tradition. And traditions are powerful because they tell students that what they're doing has been done before, that it worked, and that it's worth finishing.

One of the most telling signs that influencers had not yet done their work was a question I heard from students more times than I can count: Why do we need this? It isn't required for graduation. That question isn't a student problem. It's a communication problem. When students don't understand the value of an industry-based certification, when they see it as an optional add-on rather than a credential with real earning power and industry recognition, it tells you that the adults around them haven't made the case clearly enough. Counselors are presenting IBCs as optional rather than valuable. Teachers haven't connected the certification to a career outcome the student can see and believe in. Leaders haven't elevated IBC achievement to the same visibility as other academic milestones. The student asking "Why do we need this?" isn't the problem. The student asking that question is the symptom. The influencers around them are the answer.

One concrete strategy that extended this work beyond my district was being named CTAT Coach in Residence—a role in which I was selected to coach other CTE leaders across Texas as they progressed through the CTAT and ACTE award process. Having lived the journey myself, from the district level to the regional level to the national stage, I understood what the process required and what candidates needed to hear. Many of these leaders had accomplished remarkable things, but they didn't know how to articulate those accomplishments during interviews, panels, and presentations. We worked together to find the language for what they'd done and why it mattered. That process was itself an act of belief-building. When leaders can speak about their work with clarity and pride, it reinforces their own conviction. And when a leader walks into an interview or stands before a selection committee and owns their story, the audience believes it, too. The story is always there. Sometimes you just need someone to help you find it.

This is still a work in progress, but I'm beginning to see the shift. And it can't be driven by accountability alone. Counselors must begin presenting pathways with greater clarity and confidence—not because a metric demands it but because a student's future depends on it. Teachers must begin connecting their content to real-world applications and speaking about CTE with pride rather than apology. Leaders must begin making decisions that reflect a broader understanding of what student success actually looks like. And students will respond. Because, at the end of the day, students aren't just choosing based on what's available. They're choosing based on what the adults around them believe. When those adults believe, everything else begins to move.

PART 05

LEADING THE SYSTEM SHIFT

I — Integrate the Message | O — Own the Narrative

CHAPTER 14

ALIGNING THE MESSAGE ACROSS THE DISTRICT

Consistency creates credibility

One of the greatest obstacles to shifting perception isn't resistance—it's inconsistency. A district can have strong programs, committed leaders, and valuable opportunities, but if the message about Career and Technical Education isn't aligned across all levels, perception will remain fragmented. And fragmented perception doesn't build the kind of trust and confidence that leads to sustained change.

Students don't experience schools in parts. They experience them as a system. Each interaction contributes to how they understand what's available to them and what's valued. If the message about CTE changes depending on who's speaking, students receive mixed signals. That hesitation often leads to safer choices—choices aligned with what's consistently reinforced, even when that consistency reflects an outdated hierarchy rather than an accurate picture of opportunity.

> ***When every voice in the system tells the same story, that story becomes truth.***

One of the most powerful forms of alignment is visual. When basketball and football championship photos are displayed prominently alongside CTE Choice Awards photos, it sends a message that no policy document can replicate: These students belong in the same celebration. When the achievements of student athletes and the achievements of CTE students occupy the same wall, the same newsletter, the same stage—the hierarchy begins to flatten. Not because we minimized one to elevate the other but because we chose to see both as equally worthy of being seen.

This same principle guided how we talked about our competitive CTE student organizations. Our FFA, FCCLA, and DECA students were winning at local, state, national, and international levels, and we began treating those wins the way they deserved to be treated. Not as footnotes. As headlines. We began recognizing our CTSO champions in the same breath as our athletic champions because the message is simple: Our student athletes and our CTE students are often the same students. Their wins belong in the same conversation. In the 2024–2025 school year, 585 students were involved in career and technical student organizations—competing, leading, and representing Beaumont ISD at every level from district to international. And 66 of our top CTE students earned membership in the National Technical Honor Society, with chapters at both Beaumont United High School and West Brook High School. These are students who have demonstrated the kind of academic and technical excellence that deserves to be recognized in the same breath as any honor society in the building.

Alignment also requires visible commitment from the top. That's why our superintendent and school board members attend the CTE Choice Awards every year—sitting front and center, not as a formality but as a statement. When the most visible leaders in a district show up for something, it tells every principal, every counselor, every teacher, and every student in the room that what they're doing matters at the highest level. Leadership presence is itself a message. And that message travels further than any memo or directive ever could.

During the 2023 school year, district administrators had been assigned to provide campus support to one of our high schools. When one of the principals discovered that the core supervisors were assigned to support the other campus, his response was immediate: "If the core supervisors are over there, then what do I do if I need support from core?" And then he said it: "You all have CTE."

I was shocked. And I said it directly: "No. You have to have CTE, too. You are the instructional leader."

His statement—said without malice, said as a practical solution—revealed everything. In that principal's mind, we had CTE. His academic priority was core. Not a department that deserved the same level of instructional leadership investment as English or math. Just CTE.

That isn't a principal problem. That's a perception problem. And it lives at every level of the system, including in the offices of the very leaders responsible for championing all students and all pathways equally.

That moment reminded me that alignment work is never finished—and that it has to reach every level of the system, including the people at the top.

Ensuring that message was consistent across campuses required ongoing, intentional work. Each campus has its own culture and its own leadership. While that diversity is valuable, it can create variation in how CTE is presented and understood. We met with campus leaders regularly. We worked alongside counselors. We listened carefully to understand where misalignment existed before trying to address it. The goal was not uniformity; it was coherence. Students on every campus deserved to receive the same core message: CTE is a pathway of equal standing, connected to real outcomes, and worthy of genuine consideration.

The phrase that captures this alignment most completely is one I began saying with intention and frequency: We are all CTE. I first said it publicly in 2023 at the CTE Choice Awards, and the words have stayed with me ever since. Here's what I said that night:

> *Career and Technical Education, or CTE, is all around us, every day. You may not realize it, but the skills and knowledge that are taught through CTE programs are integral to our daily lives and the functioning of society.*
>
> *When you wake up in the morning and turn on the lights, you are benefiting from the work of electricians who have gained skills and knowledge through CTE programs. When you get dressed in the morning, the clothes you wear may have been designed by a fashion designer who learned their craft through a CTE program.*
>
> *As you go about your day, you may drive a car that was built by skilled automotive technicians who learned their trade through CTE programs. You may visit a doctor or nurse who received training through a CTE program in the field of healthcare. You may even eat food that was grown and harvested by farmers who received training in agriculture through CTE programs.*
>
> *CTE programs prepare individuals for a wide range of careers and provide them with the skills and knowledge they need to succeed in the workforce. They teach hands-on, practical skills that are essential in many industries and are in high demand by employers. CTE programs not only benefit individuals by providing them with opportunities for career advancement and financial stability, but they also benefit our society as a whole by ensuring a skilled workforce that can drive economic growth and innovation.*

CTE touches our lives every day, from the clothes we wear, to the food we eat, to the cars we drive. It provides individuals with the skills and knowledge they need to succeed in the workforce and benefits our society as a whole by ensuring a skilled and capable workforce. Tonight we recognize the importance of CTE, support its continued growth and development, and celebrate our outstanding CTE students.

That speech said what I'd been trying to say for years. We are all CTE. Everything we touch is CTE. The student who takes a business course and goes on to manage a company. The student who completes a health science pathway and becomes a nurse. The student who earns a welding certification and builds structures that outlast all of us. The student who learns culinary arts and feeds her community. Every single one of those students is CTE. And when an entire district begins to see itself that way—when the counselors, the principals, the board members, the teachers, and the students all recognize that CTE isn't a department in the corner but a thread running through every path toward a meaningful future—the perception shifts. Not gradually. Decisively.

Consistency builds credibility. When people hear the same message across different spaces, from different voices, and through different experiences, it reinforces belief. It reduces uncertainty. It builds the trust that allows perception to shift in a lasting way. Aligning the message isn't a one-time effort. It's ongoing work that requires continuous reflection, adjustment, and commitment. Because when the message is aligned, perception becomes clear. And when perception is clear, decisions become easier. Students choose with confidence. Parents support with understanding. Educators guide with clarity. That's the power of alignment.

CHAPTER 15

OWNING THE NARRATIVE BEFORE SOMEONE ELSE DOES

Proactive vs. reactive leadership

If you don't define your narrative, someone else will. That's true in business, in communities, and especially in education. In the absence of a clear, intentional message, people fill in the gaps with their own assumptions, past experiences, and incomplete understanding. Over time, those assumptions become beliefs, and those beliefs shape how decisions are made at every level of the system. Career and Technical Education has lived in that space for years. Not because it lacks value but because its story hasn't always been told clearly, consistently, or proactively.

There's a significant difference between reactive leadership and proactive leadership. Reactive leadership responds to perception. Proactive leadership shapes it. For many years, much of the work around CTE has been reactive. When enrollment declines, we promote programs; when misconceptions arise, we correct them. By the time we react, perception has already been formed.

Proactive leadership doesn't wait for the story to be told wrong. It tells the right story first.

One of the most effective ways we owned the narrative was by leveraging voices beyond our own. Our advisory council members became central to this effort. These were industry professionals who understood workforce needs firsthand, who hired employees, and who could speak directly to the value of the skills students were developing. When they spoke, people listened differently. They weren't speaking from theory. They were speaking from experience. Their voices connected CTE to real careers, real salaries, and real opportunities in a way that resonated with families in ways our own advocacy sometimes couldn't.

We also made a deliberate effort to highlight outcomes rather than just programs. We shared stories of students who had earned certifications, secured jobs, and pursued careers aligned with their training. I think about Nakisha Burns, who led our district's communications department and had been a dear friend of my sister Nasheka long before either of us ended up working in the same district. She knew me before the title. She knew where I came from. And she was proud of the direction I was taking the CTE department.

At a Chamber of Commerce event where we were showcasing CTE, another communications team member said she hadn't known about our programs until we took over the narrative—until we opened the CTE Center, invited the community in, and started telling the story publicly. That moment stopped me. If the person responsible for district communication didn't know our story, we hadn't yet owned our narrative. That wasn't an indictment of anyone. It was a clarification. And if we hadn't owned it internally, we had no foundation from which to own it externally.

What we had built was strong. But it had been the best-kept secret. And secrets don't build communities. People who know the story do.

And then there are the voices that come from completely outside your district—voices you didn't ask for, didn't prompt, and didn't expect. Linda

Creech, a curriculum consultant with iCEV who works with districts across the country, shared this after learning of my recognition:

> *I cannot think of a person more deserving. Beaumont ISD is my favorite district for good reason. Your leadership is evident all through CTE—most especially your teachers, which transfers to each student. My question each and every day is "Who even cares about children anymore?" It is a heartbreaking question that should never have to be asked. All I have to do is look to Beaumont ISD and know there is one person who cares passionately. That is you, Dr. Prudhomme. Your caring leads and guides your teachers in the art of caring. Thank you for caring about kids. For igniting that caring within each of your teachers. Exemplary CTE, teachers, and students would not be possible without you.*
>
> — **Linda Creech,** iCEV Curriculum Consultant

When someone who sees CTE departments across the entire country singles out yours as their favorite and names caring for children as the reason, that isn't a compliment. That's a narrative that has traveled far beyond your school walls and taken root in spaces you've never even entered. That's what owning your story looks like when it's working.

And then there are the moments that remind you the narrative has truly taken root—not because you planted it but because someone else tended it without being asked. Alesha Wells, one of our twenty-three CTE advisory council members and the owner of Genesis Beauty Salon, took to her personal Facebook page on IBC testing day and launched a fundraising campaign for our cosmetology students. She wasn't asked. She wasn't prompted. She simply believed in the students and decided to act. She wrote: "God has touched my heart for the Cosmetology Students at the Career Technical Center. I'm praying for those Industry Based Certifications for All Departments. This is our Future Entrepreneurs." She set a goal of $1,200 and committed that anything over that goal would be donated to the CTE Choice Awards program. She quoted John Maxwell: "People do not care how much you know until they know how much you care." That's not a community partner fulfilling an obligation. That's a community member who has been so moved by what she witnessed inside our CTE Center that she opened her own platform and her own network to support our students publicly on one of the most important days of their year. When advisory council members start showing up for your students the way coaches show up for their teams, that isn't a program milestone. That's a culture shift. And culture shifts are what this entire book is about.

In June 2025, I learned that my department was undergoing a review by an outside consultant. I wasn't included in the preliminary conversation about its purpose. That itself was a signal—a reminder that even after years of intentional work, CTE could still be defined by others in rooms where we weren't present. I could have been frustrated. And honestly, I was. But I also knew that what the review found would either validate the work or challenge it.

The findings aligned with what I'd been saying for eight years. The consultant identified that our district lacked clear processes and procedures and that students were being placed in CTE courses without following the established sequence within each program of study—course placement driven by convenience rather than intentional pathway building. At the campus level, the findings were even more direct: a complete lack of ownership of CTE coding and a lack of professional development regarding CTE programming. The consultant's conclusion was the same one I'd been drawing for nearly a decade: To improve our systems and practices, CTE must be approached as being just as important as English, math, science, and social studies. And athletics.

The consultant said what I had been saying for years. Sometimes it takes an outside voice to make the inside truth visible. Those findings weren't a surprise to me. They were a confirmation. Every pattern the consultant named was a pattern I had observed, documented, and advocated against. But perception shapes what gets heard—and sometimes the same truth lands differently depending on who's delivering it. That's not a reason to stop speaking. It's a reason to keep speaking, to keep building the record, and to welcome the moments when an outside voice gives your inside truth the platform it deserves.

That's why I want to say something directly to every CTE leader reading this book: Have your receipts. Document everything. Keep the emails. Save the meeting notes. Track the data year by year. Record the wins and the losses. Write down the moments when you were told no, when your request was denied, when your program was deprioritized, when your seat at the table was given to someone else. Not out of bitterness. Out of accountability. Because there will come a day, and it might not come quickly, when someone from the outside walks in and says what you've been saying from the inside for years. And when that day comes, you want to be able to show exactly when you said it, how many times you said it, and what the evidence looked like every step of the way. The receipts don't just protect you. They validate the work. And they tell the story that no one can dispute because you were there, you documented it, and you never stopped speaking up.

That experience also taught me something about leadership that goes beyond CTE. When you bring people to the table to evaluate a department, to assess what's working and what isn't, you have to bring the right people. Decisions made about CTE without fully understanding what CTE offers aren't solutions. They're symptoms of the same perception problem this book is about. And when outside evaluators are brought in without first talking to the people closest to the work—the coordinators, the teachers, the counselors, the students—you aren't just skipping a step. You're sending a message. You're communicating that the people who show up every day and do this work don't have a seat at the table when decisions about their work are being made. That isn't evaluation. That's a lack of trust.

And here's is what concerns me most: If a district doesn't know it has a CTE problem, it doesn't know it has a perception problem. And if it doesn't know it has a perception problem, it can't lead the solution. The people closest to the work always know. The question is whether leadership is willing to ask them—and willing to listen when they answer.

Bring the right people to the table. Trust the people who've been doing the work. And before you bring in someone from the outside to evaluate what's happening on the inside, make sure you've genuinely listened to the people who've been living it every single day.

That experience was a proactive leadership lesson delivered through a reactive moment. It reminded me that owning the narrative is never finished. It's ongoing. The moment you stop telling your story, someone else begins to define it for you. And their version may be accurate, or it may be shaped by assumptions, incomplete information, and the weight of old perception. The only protection against that is consistent, intentional, visible ownership of what you know to be true.

Owning the narrative also means addressing misconceptions directly, not defensively. When outdated perceptions arise—and they will—they must be acknowledged and replaced with a stronger, more accurate, and more compelling message. I saw this in how our work began to gain attention beyond our district. That wasn't by accident. It was the result of intentional effort to define and communicate our narrative—showing rather than just telling and ensuring that what we said about CTE was reflected in what people experienced when they encountered it.

We also saw validation at multiple levels. In 2022, Marcette Kilgore, the Texas Director of Career and Technical Education, recognized our K–8 Career Readiness initiative at the state level. That recognition confirmed something we already believed but needed the state to see. Reaching students early—before high school, before course selection, before perception had fully formed—was not just a local strategy. It was a model worth replicating. When the state's top CTE leader points to your work as an example, it sends a message to every district in Texas and to every stakeholder in your own community that what you're building matters. When we received two proclamations from the City of Beaumont recognizing CTE, those weren't just tokens of recognition. They were signals that the narrative had extended beyond school walls and taken hold in the community's sense of its own future.

The difference between reactive and proactive leadership isn't just timing. It's impact. Proactive leadership shapes what's to come. If we want CTE to be understood, valued, and chosen, we can't wait for others to define what it means. We must take ownership of that narrative, tell the story clearly, reinforce it consistently, and ensure that it's experienced in a way that reflects its true value. Because when we own the narrative, we change the conversation. And when we change the conversation, we change what people believe.

PART

06

NORMALIZING CTE

N — Normalize CTE as a First Choice

CHAPTER 16

WHEN PERCEPTION CHANGES, EVERYTHING CHANGES

Enrollment, outcomes, and belief

There's a moment in every system shift when the results begin to show. Not all at once, and not always in dramatic ways, but steadily and consistently. Conversations begin to feel different. Decisions begin to look different. What once required constant effort begins to happen more naturally. That moment doesn't come from simply adding more programs or increasing promotion. It comes from something deeper. It comes from changing perception.

The growth we've seen isn't just in certifications and signing ceremonies. It's in the programs themselves. Our STEM offerings have expanded significantly—from Robotics I through Advanced Engineering Practicum courses, from Computer Science I through AP Computer Science, from a single engineering pathway to a comprehensive STEM sequence that connects directly to the industries and employers that make Southeast Texas run. When perception shifts, programs grow. When programs grow, more students have access to more pathways. And when more students have access, the numbers follow. That's not a coincidence. That's alignment.

Enrollment is often the first place people look for evidence of success, because it's the most visible and measurable indicator. But enrollment isn't just a number. It's a reflection of belief. When students believe in the value of a pathway, they choose it. When they don't, they hesitate. When we tied the state of Texas in industry-based certifications and then surpassed them in Level 1 certifications, that achievement didn't come from a campaign. It came from students who were invested, who believed in what they were doing, who committed to completing pathways and earning credentials because the environment around them had communicated that those credentials were real, valuable, and worth pursuing.

When students believe in the pathway, they don't just enroll. They invest.

The numbers tell a story of sustained growth. According to the 2024–2025 Texas Academic Performance Report reflecting outcomes from the 2023–2024 school year, Beaumont ISD demonstrated remarkable progress in College, Career, and Military Readiness—with 78.4 percent of annual graduates meeting CCMR readiness criteria. That's not a statistic. That's a graduating class walking across a stage prepared for what comes next. And it didn't happen by accident. It happened because students believed in their pathways enough to complete them and because the system around them had finally begun communicating that those pathways were worth completing.

Every certification earned, every Level I credential completed, and every student who crossed that graduation stage career ready was proof that high-demand, high-skill, and high-wage weren't just taglines. They were the result.

To put that in concrete terms, in the 2023–2024 school year, BISD's industry-based certification results for College, Career, and Military Readiness came in at 34.9 percent, matching the state of Texas at 34.9 percent. And in Level I and

Level II certificates, we didn't just match the state. We surpassed it, achieving 8.1 percent compared to the state average of 1.1 percent. Eight times the state average. Let that land for a moment. Our students earned 126 Level 1 certifications in a single year—college-level credentials earned before graduation. On Career or Military Readiness, BISD reached 42 percent compared to the state's 38 percent. And in US Armed Forces enlistment, BISD students enlisted at a rate of 2.5 percent compared to the state's 1.8 percent. These aren't soft metrics. These are state-validated measures of student readiness, and Beaumont ISD is leading on every one of them. A district that was still fighting for its seat at the table, still advocating for IBC testing to appear on the district calendar, still pushing for CTE teachers to be recognized at convocation, produced outcomes that exceeded the state of Texas. The programs were never the problem. They never were. And the numbers finally said it loud enough for everyone to hear.

The numbers aren't just a snapshot of where we are. They're a foundation for where we're going. Beaumont ISD has set a formal performance objective to increase the percent of students who earn an industry-based certification from 23 percent to 43 percent by August 2030. And the district's CCMR goal targets an increase from 65 percent to 90 percent of graduates meeting the criteria for College, Career, and Military Readiness by that same year. These aren't aspirational statements. They are board-level commitments. When a school board sets a target of 43 percent IBC attainment and you're already at 34.9 percent, that isn't a district that's ignoring CTE. That's a district that's beginning to structure itself around what CTE can deliver. The perception is shifting. And the goals are starting to reflect it.

The shift in perception shows up most visibly in what students are walking away with. The green cords our seniors receive at the CTE Choice Awards, earned through industry-based certifications recognized by employers at the local, state, and national level, are not ceremonial. They're credentials. They represent assessments, examinations, licenses, and trainings administered by the same industries that are actively hiring our graduates. When Alicia Green leads that cording ceremony each year, she isn't just recognizing students. She's changing what the community believes is possible inside a CTE classroom. And when those same students cross the graduation stage wearing that dark green cord alongside their diploma, the community sees something it can't unsee: a graduate who isn't just diploma ready. They're career ready. Those dark green cords have become a staple in Beaumont ISD CTE. Students know about them. They want them. And when a student is working toward a cord, when the credential becomes something they're chasing rather than something we're pushing, that's the clearest sign that the perception has shifted. They aren't enrolling because we asked them to. They're enrolling because they believe in what it leads to.

The impact has extended beyond our own district. Neighboring districts have incorporated the IBC cording concept, recognizing that visible, wearable symbols of achievement change how students see themselves and how communities see CTE. A student who earns both a green cord and a copper cord is walking across that graduation stage with visible proof that they aren't just certified in a skilled trade. They're recognized by the state of Texas as college, career, and military ready. Two cords. Two credentials. One student who chose CTE and let it take them exactly where it promised.

Students who earn their CCMR point also become eligible for the BISD Plus program, which allows early release or late arrival during their senior year. That isn't just a perk. It's a structural reward built into the system that says, if you earned your career readiness credential, the district trusts you with your time. That kind of structural recognition changes how students see the value of what they've earned.

Business partners. Community leaders. People who lived in this city, who sent their children to these schools, who had driven past the CTE Center hundreds of times. They didn't know. Not because it was hidden but because it had never been told. In that moment, the work became undeniable. We didn't have a program problem. We had a perception problem. And the moment we decided to stop keeping that secret was the moment everything began to move.

Think about what CTE actually encompasses. We have business and industry engagement, CTE partners, and FFA students competing at state levels. DECA students winning at state and international levels. FCCLA students winning regional and national competitions. Students competing at the Houston Rodeo in agricultural and technical categories. Teams representing their district in competitions that require the kind of technical mastery and professional skill that few academic programs can replicate. We aren't talking about electives. We're talking about excellence. And when that excellence is visible, when it's recognized alongside athletic championships, when it's celebrated in the same spaces and with the same energy, people begin to understand something they hadn't not understood before: We are all CTE. Everything we touch is CTE. The doctor was in a health science pathway. The contractor built skills in construction technology. The business owner learned in a marketing or finance program. CTE isn't a separate track. It's the foundation beneath almost every career that exists.

One of the clearest indicators that perception had shifted was what began happening inside our programs themselves. Our junior and senior courses at the CTE Center are dually enrolled with Lamar Institute of Technology (LIT) and Lamar State College Orange (LSCO). That means students aren't just earning high school credit. They're earning college credit. They graduate from high school already holding their Level I certificate—a credential that positions them for immediate employment or advanced study in their field before they ever walk across a graduation stage. That's not a promise. That's a result. And it's the kind of result that changes how students, parents, and employers understand what CTE offers.

At the 2025 CTE Choice Awards, we introduced a moment that captured everything this work has been building toward: the Workforce Ready Signing. Modeled after the athletic signing ceremonies that communities celebrate with pride, the Workforce Ready Signing recognizes graduating seniors who have been offered conditional employment directly related to their CTE program of study and the industry-based certifications they earned. Students came forward to signing tables and put pen to paper on Certificates of Intent—real conditional job offers from real employers.

Fourteen students signed with Acadian Ambulance as EMTs, hired directly out of the health science pathway by the very company their instructor also works for. One student, who had spent the year as an intern at a local pharmacy, was offered a position as a pharmacy technician in training. His employer said he absorbs everything they teach him, he's punctual and determined to succeed, and he performs his tasks to the high standard they hold for patient care. Six auto technology students received conditional employment offers from Bechtel—one of the largest engineering, construction, and project management companies in the world—making Beaumont ISD the first district to receive Bechtel job training and career offers for high school graduates. Boot Barn donated safety-approved work boots to each student. These young men didn't just sign for a job. They signed for a career in an industry that builds the infrastructure of this country before they ever walked across a graduation stage. Six students received full trade scholarships from Associated Builders and Contractors Southeast Texas, covering a full year of tuition for the craft of their choosing in the oil, gas, and chemical industries—industries that are the economic backbone of Southeast Texas.

That night wasn't a ceremony. It was a demonstration. Every student who walked to those signing tables was proof that CTE works when the system believes in it. They hadn't just taken courses. They had built pathways. They had earned certifications. They had completed internships. And industry had noticed. Employers didn't not show up at the CTE Choice Awards to be polite.

They showed up because they wanted what our students had built. That's what happens when perception changes. The community stops asking whether CTE is valuable and starts asking how to get their students into it.

On April 1, 2026, I received a message from the communications department announcing that the Celebration of Excellence Gala would feature a new recognition: the BISD Staff Excellence Award. Each principal and department head was being asked to nominate a non-teacher employee. All nominations would go to a committee, and the winner would be recognized at the gala.

I'll be honest. My first thought was that it was an April fools' joke.

It wasn't. And when I sat with it for a moment, I realized what it actually was. It was the CTE Choice Awards philosophy—the idea that everyone who contributes to student success deserves to be seen, named, and celebrated—finding its way into the district's highest recognition event. We hadn't lobbied for it. We hadn't suggested it. We had simply built something visible enough, meaningful enough, and replicable enough that the district decided to bring that spirit into its own celebration.

That's what happens when perception changes. The model you built in the margins eventually moves to the main stage.

Parents respond to shifts in perception. As visibility increased and outcomes became clearer in our community, parents moved from hesitation to support, from uncertainty to advocacy. Educators respond, as well. When teachers, counselors, and leaders see the impact of CTE through student success and system alignment, their mindset continues to deepen.

This alignment among students, parents, and educators creates a unified system where decisions are supported at every level and the narrative reinforces itself. When perception changes, everything changes. And that's when the work begins to sustain itself—not through constant effort but through alignment that has become embedded in the culture of the system.

Visibility at the highest level of the system requires intentionality, too. As a district, each department is required to contribute to the monthly board reports and to the superintendent's mid-year and end-of-year reports—showcasing accomplishments, documenting progress, and keeping the board and district leadership informed about what's happening inside every department. We took that responsibility seriously. Every month. Every report. Every opportunity to put CTE accomplishments in front of the people responsible for setting the direction of this district was an opportunity we used. Because if the board doesn't see the results, if the superintendent's report doesn't include what CTE students are earning, competing for, and being hired to do, then the perception problem lives even at the governance level. Data that isn't reported is data that doesn't exist in the minds of decision makers. And decision makers who don't see CTE results can't be expected to champion CTE priorities. So, we reported. Consistently. Thoroughly. And without apology.

CHAPTER 17

MAKING CTE A FIRST CHOICE, NOT A SECOND OPTION

The ultimate goal

The ultimate goal of this work is not simply to improve programs, increase enrollment, or expand opportunities. Those outcomes matter, but they're not the end goal. The goal is deeper. It's to shift Career and Technical Education from being seen as a secondary option to being recognized and selected as a first choice.

For too long, CTE has been positioned, often unintentionally, as an alternative rather than a primary pathway. Even when programs are strong and outcomes are clear, the perception remains that CTE is something students settle for rather than something they aspire to. That perception must change. Because when a pathway is viewed as a second option, it will always struggle to reach its full potential. Students will hesitate. Parents will question. Educators will present it with caution rather than confidence.

Making CTE a first choice begins with how we define success. In many school systems, success has been narrowly defined around college acceptance, test scores, and academic achievement. Expanding that definition isn't a concession—it's an act of leadership. Success must include multiple pathways, must reflect the reality that students have different interests and strengths, and must acknowledge that meaningful careers, strong incomes, and fulfilled lives can be achieved through a variety of routes.

When we expand our definition of success, we expand the number of students who believe they can achieve it.

My son received an incredible job offer during his college graduation ceremony. My daughter— a CTE student who turned an entrepreneurship and small business credential into brand deals and a Netflix casting opportunity before her sophomore year of college—is living proof that when students are given both access and belief, they don't just succeed. They exceed. Those aren't exceptions. Those are examples of what becomes possible when the pathway is real, the belief is consistent, and the system gets out of the way and lets students become who they were always meant to be.

During my CTAT Administrator of the Year interview, I remember being asked, "What does a typical CTE student look like to you?" For me, that was a two-fold question because the answer looks very different depending on when you ask it.

In the past, I would have described Adria Flowers, a 2002 graduate of Ozen High School who always wanted to be a veterinarian. She gave a kindergarten speech about animals, and when her mother, Elvena Colbert, showed that video at Adria's graduation celebration from Tuskegee University, College of Veterinary Medicine, it warmed my heart in a way I'll never forget. Was the path easy for Adria? I'm sure she had bumps along the way. There were moments when she wanted to give up. And I remember her mother being right there, providing encouragement even when it felt like Adria had lost her passion. Today, Adria has her own private veterinary practice in Houston, Texas. She got there without a clearly defined Level 1 through Level 4 pathway. Without technical dual credit. Without work-based learning placements embedded in her program. Without the industry connections and CTSO competitions and FFA scholarships that exist today. She got there on passion alone. And that was enough.

Today, a typical CTE student looks different—not because the passion has changed but because the support around that passion has. A student who walks into our Agriculture program with the same dream Adria had at five years old doesn't have to find their own way. They have a clear, defined pathway from Level 1 through Level 4, starting with Principles of Agriculture, Food, and Natural Resources in ninth grade and building all the way through Veterinary Science, Advanced Animal Science, and the Practicum in Agriculture, Food, and Natural Resources in twelfth grade. Along the way, that student can earn the Elanco Fundamentals of Animal Science Certification, the Certified Veterinary Assistant Level 1 credential, and shadow an animal scientist in a biology lab or intern in a veterinary clinic as part of their work-based learning experience. They can compete in an FFA agriscience fair. They can earn college credit through dual enrollment. And when they graduate, they can walk directly into an apprenticeship as a Reproduction Technician, pursue an associate's degree in biological and physical sciences, or continue toward a bachelor's in animal science or zoology—with a median veterinarian wage of over $125,000 waiting at the end of the road. Adria had the passion. Today's students have the passion *and* the pathway. That combination is unstoppable.

But here's what hasn't changed. Here's the one constant across every era, every program, and every student who has ever sat in a CTE classroom: You needed passion then, and you need passion right now. The structure can guide you. The pathway can support you. The certifications can credential you. But passion is what gets you through the hard days. Passion is what keeps you in the program when it gets difficult. Passion is what drives you all the way to a private veterinary practice in Houston, or a job offer at graduation, or a Netflix casting opportunity before your sophomore year of college. Passion was always the foundation. Everything we've built is designed to give that passion somewhere to go.

Normalization is the ultimate indicator of success. When CTE is no longer treated as a separate track but as an integrated part of how we think about learning, opportunity, and future readiness, something fundamental shifts. Scheduling allows students to pursue multiple pathways without unnecessary barriers. Messaging reinforces CTE as part of a comprehensive educational experience. Recognition elevates CTE achievements alongside academic accomplishments without hierarchy. Leadership models the belief through decisions, through advocacy, and through the way CTE is represented in every conversation about the future of students and communities.

When these elements are aligned, CTE becomes normalized. And when something is normalized, it no longer feels like an exception. It becomes expected. It becomes understood. It becomes part of how decisions are made. This is where the shift from second option to first choice happens. Not through convincing students to choose CTE but through creating an environment where choosing CTE feels natural, respected, and wise. Where students pursue it not because it was the only door open to them but because it was the door that aligned most clearly with who they are and who they intend to become. Scheduling shouldn't be English, math, science, social studies, athletics—and then CTE. CTE belongs in that conversation from the very beginning.

I think about Theron Brown. He was one of my daughter's friends—someone she had known since elementary school, who had grown up in the same community, walked the same halls, and sat in the same classrooms as the students I'd spent years trying to reach. I encountered him during a CTE walk in the second semester of his senior year. I asked him what he planned to do after graduation. He told me directly: College was not for him. He was going to trade school to become an electrical lineman. Electrical linemen install and repair electrical power systems—high-skill, high-demand, essential work that keeps the lights on across every community in this country. He knew exactly what he wanted. He had made his decision with clarity and confidence. And I was proud of him—not in spite of his choice but because of it. He enrolled in the program. He completed it within a semester. His family threw him a graduation party. My daughter and their friends were there to celebrate him. And today he is working full time. That isn't a consolation story. That's a success story. And the only difference between Theron's story being celebrated and being dismissed is whether the adults around him believed that what he chose was worth choosing. They did. And so did he.

In my journey from a CTE teacher who just wanted scissors, file folders, and ink pens to the 2026 ACTE National Administrator of the Year standing on a national stage, this has always been about one thing: making sure that every student who walks through a CTE door believes that the door they chose was worth choosing. I believed it then. I believe it now. And I'll keep believing it—loudly, consistently, and without waiting for permission.

CONCLUSION
THE WORK AHEAD

Grounded. Honest. A call to lead differently.

If there's one truth that remains after everything you've read, it should be this: The work ahead is not about fixing Career and Technical Education. It's about changing how it's seen. CTE isn't broken. What it has lacked, for too long, is alignment between what it is and how it is perceived. And that's a leadership issue. Because perception is shaped by systems, and systems are shaped by leaders.

This work begins with awareness, but it's sustained through ownership. At some point, every leader has to decide whether they'll simply operate within the system or take responsibility for how that system is experienced. For me, that realization showed up in the way people responded to me over time. I would walk into the human resources department, and before I could even say why I was there, the executive director of human resources, Derwin Samuels, would smile and say, "Dr. Prudhomme . . . what do you need for CTE now?" It was said with familiarity and warmth because he knew exactly what it meant. He knew that when I showed up, I was advocating. That became part of my identity as a leader, not because I set out to create that reputation but because consistency creates recognition. And recognition creates momentum.

When I stepped into this role, I made a deliberate decision to celebrate CTE Month every February—intentionally, visibly, and without apology. I've said it before and I'll say it again: Toot your own horn. Not out of pride but out of responsibility. Because if we don't tell our story, it won't be told. And what remains unseen is rarely valued.

This work requires honesty—a willingness to acknowledge that we've contributed to the perceptions we're now trying to change, not intentionally but through systems, structures, and messaging that were never fully aligned. It requires consistency because perception isn't shaped in a moment. It requires patience because change doesn't happen overnight. And it requires courage—the courage to challenge long-standing beliefs, to question systems that have been in place for years, to speak differently, act differently, and lead differently.

I think about that senior English teacher who looked at me in the front office all those years ago and said, "You think you're important." What she didn't remember was that she was one of my English teachers when I was a student at West Brook. She had taught me in those same halls. And years later, I was standing in front of her as a colleague—as a CTE teacher returning to the building that had shaped me—over a supply order for scissors, file folders, and ink pens. I don't carry that moment with bitterness. I carry it as a reminder. Because every CTE teacher who has ever felt invisible in their own building deserves to hear what Selwyn Jones said that day: "She *is* important." You are important. And the work you do is worth showing up for—every single day.

Lydia Sylvester, our director of guidance and counseling, reached out after the national award was announced and said something I needed to hear: "I hope you're taking some time to take it all in." People who are driven by purpose rarely stop long enough to receive what they've earned. To every director of CTE reading this book: That message is for you, too. Take it in. The certifications earned. The students who stayed the course. The teachers who believed before anyone else did. The partnerships that took years to build. You've been doing this work in rooms where not everyone understood its value. Take a moment to receive what you've built. And then keep going.

A principal I worked for early in my career had a saying he came back to often. Whenever someone was quick to point the finger at a student, a parent, a teacher, or a system, he would stop the conversation and say it plainly: "When you point one finger at someone, you have three pointing back at you."

I've carried that saying with me for decades. And I want to leave it with you here because it's the most honest thing I can say to every education leader reading this book. It's easy to point at the scheduling system. It's easy to point at the counselors, the principals, the parents, the community. But every finger pointed outward has three pointing back. We built this perception together—through systems we inherited, decisions we made, and messages we sent without realizing it. And we're the ones responsible for changing it.

Not someone else. Us.

The 2025–2026 school year began with Beaumont ISD's theme: "All In All Year." Dr. Allen's charge was clear: Everyone in Beaumont ISD was to be all in, all year. And I sat with that for a moment. Because for eight years, that's exactly what I'd been asking. Not just from my team. From the system. From the schools. From the people with the power to make CTE a priority. All in. All year. I couldn't help but wonder, *When are we going to get the message?* And then I looked around at what had been built, at what the data was showing, at what the community was beginning to say, and I thought, *Maybe we finally are.*

Think about the student I described at the very beginning of this book. The one being directed away from Career and Technical Education—not because CTE isn't a good fit but because the story being told is the wrong one. That student is waiting for a different story. For a counselor who presents pathways with confidence. For a system that celebrates all forms of achievement. For a community that understands what CTE actually is and what it actually leads to.

That student is the reason for this work. And that student is within reach of a different outcome—if we're willing to lead differently. We are all CTE. Everything we touch is CTE.

That's the work ahead. And it begins with how we choose to lead.

—Dr. Donna Prudhomme

APPENDIX

FROM INSIGHT TO IMPLEMENTATION

Positioning Leaders to Take Action

This appendix is designed to move you from understanding to execution. Throughout this book, you've explored how perception shapes decisions, how systems influence belief, and how leadership determines whether Career and Technical Education is seen as a first choice or a second option.

Now the question becomes, What do you do next?

The following tools are designed to help you assess your current reality, identify areas for growth, and begin implementing intentional strategies that shift perception across your district.

APPENDIX A

THE P.E.R.C.E.P.T.I.O.N. SHIFT™ AUDIT TOOL

Leaders Assess Their District

Before you can change perception, you must understand your current state. This audit is designed to help you identify where your district stands and where alignment is needed. This isn't about judgment. It's about awareness, and awareness is the first step toward intentional leadership.

P — Position the Truth

Do people clearly understand what CTE is and what it leads to?

- Is CTE presented as a pathway or as an option?
- Can students clearly articulate what CTE leads to after graduation?
- Are outcomes—certifications, careers, wages—consistently communicated across campuses?

If students, parents, or staff cannot clearly explain the value of CTE, perception is likely unclear. The work begins here.

E — Examine the Current Narrative

What are people currently saying about CTE?

- What do counselors say when advising students about pathway options?
- What language do teachers use when discussing CTE in the classroom?
- What do parents believe about these programs, and where did that belief come from?

Perception is revealed in everyday language. Listen carefully to what's said—and what's left unsaid.

R — Reveal the Hidden Messages

What are students actually experiencing?

- Are certain pathways easier to access than others in your scheduling structure?
- What is celebrated publicly—and what is quietly overlooked?
- What do students believe about who "belongs" in CTE?

Students respond to experience, not intention. The gap between what you intend and what students experience is where perception lives.

C — Clarify the Value

Is the value of CTE consistently communicated?

- Are CTE outcomes connected to real career data and earning potential?
- Are industry partnerships visible to students, parents, and the community?
- Are success stories shared regularly in the same spaces as academic achievements?

If value isn't visible, it won't be understood. Clarity requires repetition.

E — Elevate Awareness

Who knows about your programs—and who doesn't?

- Are parents informed about CTE pathways before their children begin high school?
- Are community members aware of the outcomes your programs produce?
- Do business partners understand the impact of your programs on workforce readiness?

If key stakeholders are unaware, perception remains limited. And limited perception limits decisions.

P — Prioritize Access

Can all students realistically participate?

- Are there scheduling conflicts that force students to choose between CTE and academic courses?
- Are pathways accessible to all student groups, including high-achieving students?
- Are there logistical barriers—transportation, location, program availability—that limit participation?

Access must be real, not assumed. A door that's hard to open is effectively closed.

T — Train the Influencers

Do staff believe in CTE and communicate that belief with confidence?

- Are counselors fully informed about CTE pathways, certifications, and outcomes?

- Do teachers connect their content to career relevance and reinforce pathway value?
- Are leaders aligned in their messaging about CTE as a priority?

Students follow belief. If the adults in the room are uncertain, students will be, too.

I — Integrate the Message

Is CTE part of the district narrative or separate from it?

- Is CTE included in district presentations, strategic plans, and board communications?
- Is it visible in communication with families across all campuses consistently?
- Is it embedded in how the district defines and celebrates student success?

Integration creates normalization. When CTE is woven into the fabric of the district story, it stops being a program and becomes a pathway.

O — Own the Narrative

Are you leading the message or reacting to it?

- Are you proactively sharing CTE stories, data, and outcomes before misconceptions arise?
- Are common misconceptions about CTE addressed directly and confidently?
- Are outcomes consistently shared with the community, not just within the school system?

If you aren't defining the narrative, someone else is. Proactive storytelling is a leadership responsibility.

N — Normalize CTE

Is CTE seen as a first choice in your district?

- Do high-achieving students enroll in CTE programs, and are their stories visible?
- Do parents support CTE pathways with confidence rather than hesitation?
- Do staff present CTE with the same pride and urgency as other pathways?

Normalization is the ultimate indicator of success. When CTE is no longer an exception, the shift is complete.

APPENDIX B

CTE MESSAGING & VISIBILITY CHECKLIST

Immediate Action Steps

This checklist is designed for quick implementation. These are actions you can begin immediately to increase visibility and shift perception.

VISIBILITY

- Showcase CTE programs monthly, not just during CTE Month or annual events
- Highlight student success stories consistently across all communication channels
- Host open house events that invite community members to see programs firsthand
- Bring CTE experiences to K–8 campuses through career readiness initiatives
- Ensure CTE is prominently visible on district and campus websites and social media
- Display CTE student work and certifications alongside academic achievements in hallways

MESSAGING

- Replace "option" language with "pathway" language in all communications
- Connect every program description to specific career outcomes and earning potential
- Share salary data and workforce demand statistics clearly and regularly
- Align messaging across all campuses so students receive a consistent narrative
- Train staff on how to communicate CTE value with confidence and specificity
- Eliminate language that positions CTE as a backup or alternative plan

RECOGNITION

- Celebrate industry-based certification achievements publicly and consistently
- Recognize CTE teachers alongside academic teachers at district events
- Announce IBC results the same way STAAR results are announced
- Create signature events—such as a CTE awards ceremony—that honor student achievement
- Highlight CTE student and teacher accomplishments at school board meetings
- Feature CTE alumni successes in community communications and local media

COMMUNITY ENGAGEMENT

- Invite business and industry partners into classrooms regularly, not just for career day
- Allow advisory council members to speak publicly about CTE's workforce value

- ✦ Partner with industry for work-based learning and real-world exposure opportunities
- ✦ Share student success stories with local media on a consistent schedule
- ✦ Pursue community recognition and proclamations that extend the CTE narrative beyond school walls

STUDENT EXPERIENCE

- ✦ Provide early exposure through K–8 career readiness programming
- ✦ Create hands-on learning opportunities that go beyond a single career day event
- ✦ Ensure students can see themselves in CTE through representation in marketing and stories
- ✦ Reinforce the connection between classroom learning and real career outcomes at every level
- ✦ Remove scheduling barriers that force students to choose between CTE and academic courses
- ✦ • Implement structured coaching programs that develop CTE leaders and educators in the art of telling their own story.

APPENDIX C

DISTRICT IMPLEMENTATION ROADMAP

From Awareness to Transformation

This roadmap outlines how to implement the P.E.R.C.E.P.T.I.O.N. Shift™ over time. Perception doesn't change in a single school year. This is a multi-year commitment that requires intentional leadership at every phase.

Phase 1: Awareness (Months 1–3)

Focus: Understand your current reality.

- ✦ Conduct the full P.E.R.C.E.P.T.I.O.N. Shift™ audit across your district
- ✦ Identify gaps in perception, access, and messaging
- ✦ Gather honest feedback from students, parents, and staff about their CTE experience
- ✦ Assess current messaging, visibility practices, and recognition patterns

Phase 2: Alignment (Months 3–6)

Focus: Ensure everyone is communicating the same message.

- ✦ Train counselors, teachers, and campus leaders on CTE value and communication

- Align messaging across all campuses around a unified narrative
- Begin consistent, intentional visibility efforts; do not wait for a perfect plan
- Start recognizing CTE achievements alongside academic accomplishments publicly

Phase 3: Activation (Months 6–12)

Focus: Make CTE visible and understood.

- Launch visibility campaigns—CTE Month celebrations, community events, media outreach
- Expand student exposure through K–8 career readiness and campus demonstrations
- Increase community engagement through advisory councils and industry partnerships
- Highlight success stories consistently in multiple formats and channels

Phase 4: Integration (Year 2)

Focus: Make CTE part of the system, not separate from it.

- Embed CTE into the district's identity, strategic plan, and definition of student success
- Align scheduling and program placement decisions to expand access and reduce barriers
- Normalize recognition of CTE achievements alongside academic accomplishments
- Ensure consistency across all campuses in how CTE is presented and supported

Phase 5: Transformation (Year 3+)

Focus: Sustain the shift.

- CTE becomes a first-choice pathway chosen with confidence, not as a backup
- Enrollment reflects belief-driven decisions, not recruitment-driven campaigns
- Staff mindset is aligned, and CTE advocacy is embedded in the school culture
- Community understanding is strong, and the district's CTE narrative is self-sustaining

APPENDIX D

THE CAREER PIPELINE FRAMEWORK™

Grade 7 through Postsecondary

The Career Pipeline Framework™ is a structured, sequential model that maps the full career development journey from middle school through postsecondary. It's designed to ensure that every student—regardless of grade level—is intentionally exposed to, prepared for, and supported through career pathways that align with their interests, strengths, and goals. The framework begins with identity and awareness and ends with successful transition into college, career, or military service.

Career Discovery → Career Exploration → Career Foundation → Career Skills → Career Application → Career Credential → Career Launch

CAREER IDENTITY: MIDDLE SCHOOL

Career Discovery (Grade 7)

Focus: Identity Building & Awareness

- Strengths and interest discovery
- Introduction to career clusters

- Foundational employability skills
- Real-world career connections

Outcome: Students begin forming career identity and awareness.

Career Exploration (Grade 8)

Focus: Pathway Exposure & Alignment

- Exploration of specific career pathways
- Industry guest speakers and simulations
- Career interest assessments
- Pathway selection guidance

Outcome: Students identify potential career pathways aligned to their interests.

CAREER READINESS: HIGH SCHOOL

Career Foundation (Grade 9)

Focus: Foundational Industry Knowledge

- Industry fundamentals
- Safety, ethics, and compliance
- Technical terminology
- Career readiness fundamentals

Outcome: Students establish foundational industry knowledge and workplace expectations.

Career Skills (Grade 10)

Focus: Technical Skill Development

- Hands-on labs and simulations
- Applied industry projects

- Technology and tool integration
- Performance-based assessments

Outcome: Students demonstrate core technical competencies.

Career Application (Grade 11)

Focus: Real-World Experience

- Work-based learning
- Internships and practicum
- Capstone projects

Outcome: Students perform authentic industry tasks with increasing independence.

Career Credential (Grade 12)

Focus: Certification & Workforce Readiness

- Industry-based certification preparation
- Dual credit and postsecondary alignment
- Resume and interview readiness
- Professional portfolio development

Outcome: Students earn industry credentials and demonstrate workforce readiness.

CAREER LAUNCH: POSTSECONDARY

Career Launch (Postsecondary)

Focus: Workforce & Postsecondary Placement

- College enrollment
- Technical training programs
- Registered apprenticeships

- Military service
- Direct workforce entry

Outcome: Successful transition into college, career, or military service.

The Career Pipeline Framework™

Designed by Dr. Donna Prudhomme

www.drdonnaprudhomme.com

A FINAL NOTE

This work doesn't happen by accident. It requires intentional leadership, aligned systems, and a clear understanding of how perception is shaped and sustained. The districts that see the greatest and most lasting success aren't necessarily those with the most programs. They are those with the most alignment between what they offer and how it's understood, between what they say and what students experience, between the value they know CTE has and the value the community finally begins to see.

If you're ready to move from awareness to implementation, the next step isn't to do more. It's to lead differently. To ask harder questions. To listen more carefully. To align more deliberately. And to tell the story of Career and Technical Education—your story—with the confidence and conviction it deserves.

That's where transformation begins.

—Dr. Donna Prudhomme

BIBLIOGRAPHY

This book draws primarily from the author's own lived experience across more than three decades in education—as a CTE teacher, high school counselor, high school assistant principal and magnet school coordinator, high school principal, and director of Career and Technical Education. The stories, strategies, and observations shared throughout are her own.

The following outside sources are referenced in this book:

Greene, Robert. *The 48 Laws of Power*. Penguin Books, 1998. Law 45—"Preach the Need for Change but Never Reform Too Much at Once"—is referenced in Chapter Two as a framework for understanding why perception change must be intentional, gradual, and sustained rather than sweeping and sudden.

Meyer, Danny. *Setting the Table: The Transforming Power of Hospitality in Business.* HarperCollins, 2006. The concept of enlightened hospitality is referenced in Chapter Four as a framework for understanding why student perception of CTE is shaped by experience and feeling, not program quality alone.

Natario, Nick. "Gallery Furniture Opens Trade School to Help Houstonians Learn New Skills and Land a Job." *ABC13 Houston*, October 23, 2020. Retrieved from https://abc13.com/post/gallery-furniture-mattress-mack-launches-trade-school-to-help-houstonians-helping-learn-new-skills-land-a-job/7250092/ This report on Gallery Furniture's trade school initiative, launched by Houston's own Mattress Mack, provided a real-world example of how industry leaders are stepping in to fill workforce gaps—informing the discussion of community and employer partnerships in Chapter Six.

Serhant, Ryan. *Brand It Like Serhant: The Proven System for Building Your Personal Brand and Winning in Any Market*. Hachette Book Group, 2024. The principle that visibility is the foundation of value—"If people don't see it, it doesn't exist"—informed the discussion of CTE branding and presence in Chapter Seven.

Texas Education Agency. Definition of CTE Completer. Retrieved from the Texas Education Agency official guidance on Career and Technical Education program of study completion requirements. Referenced in Chapter Twelve.

Texas Education Agency. *Texas Academic Performance Report 2024-2025.* Retrieved from https://rptsvr1.tea.texas.gov/perfreport/tapr/tapr_srch.html?year=2025&lev=D.

Data referenced in this book is drawn from the Texas Academic Performance Report (TAPR), published annually by the Texas Education Agency (TEA). TAPR data reflects outcomes from the prior school year. All data cited in this book reflects the 2023–2024 school year and was retrieved from the 2024–2025 TAPR.

Additional data is drawn from the *Beaumont Independent School District CTE Year in Review 2024-2025*, produced by the Beaumont ISD Department of Career and Technical Education, updated February 2026.

The following sources are referenced in this book as historical documentation of Career and Technical Education programs and student organizations in Beaumont ISD:

Clifton J. Ozen Magnet High School Yearbook. 2011. Documents the first Ozen Oscars academic achievement celebration held on December 16, 2010, in the Ozen Band Hall. Referenced in Chapter Seven.

Clifton J. Ozen Magnet High School Yearbook. 2014. Documents the Video Technology Hollywood trip and Panther Productions program led by Camille Briggs. Referenced in Chapter Seven.

Family, Career and Community Leaders of America. "History." FCCLA National Organization. Retrieved from https://fcclainc.org/about/history. Future Homemakers of America was founded on June 11, 1945. The name was officially changed to Family, Career and Community Leaders of America in July 1999 when voting delegates at the National Leadership Conference in Boston, Massachusetts approved the proposed name change. Referenced in Chapter Two.

The Smith-Hughes National Vocational Education Act of 1917 is referenced in Chapter Two as historical documentation of the legislative foundation of vocational education in the United States and its role in shaping the gendered and class-based perception of Career and Technical Education.

West Brook High School Yearbook. 2000. The story of Elizabeth Spell and her participation in the Future Farmers of America—including her awards, competitions, and personal reflection on leadership and self-confidence—is drawn from this source and is referenced in Chapter Six.

West Brook High School Yearbook. 2000. The account of Future Homemakers of America transitioning to Family, Career and Community Leaders of America—including the organizational name change, its purpose, and the mission statement of the updated organization—is drawn from this source and is referenced in Chapter Two.

ABOUT THE AUTHOR

DR. DONNA PRUDHOMME

Dr. Donna Prudhomme is a nationally-recognized leader in Career and Technical Education known for transforming how schools, districts, and communities understand and value career pathways. With more than three decades of experience in education and industry, she has served as a teacher, counselor, assistant principal, principal, and district leader—bringing a rare, comprehensive perspective to the work of preparing students for life beyond graduation.

She currently serves as the Director of Career and Technical Education for Beaumont Independent School District in Texas, where she has led a districtwide transformation of CTE programs through strategic expansion, intentional rebranding, and strong industry partnerships. Under her leadership, Beaumont ISD has significantly increased student access to high-quality programs and industry-based certifications, positioning CTE as a central driver of student success and College, Career, and Military Readiness.

In recognition of her impact, Dr. Prudhomme was named the Association for Career and Technical Education 2026 National Administrator of the Year, one of the highest honors in the field. She was also named the 2025 ACTE Region IV Administrator of the Year and the 2024 CTAT Texas Administrator of the Year. She was featured in *EdTech Focus on K–12* Magazine, Spring 2026, for her leadership in Career and Technical Education.

Dr. Prudhomme's leadership is marked not only by outcomes but by vision. She is known for creating innovative initiatives such as the Annual CTE Choice Awards, a red-carpet celebration that brings together students, educators, and community partners to elevate and honor the impact of Career and Technical Education.

A committed lifelong learner, she holds multiple advanced degrees from Lamar University, Prairie View A&M University, and Nova Southeastern University, and is certified as a superintendent, principal, school counselor, and vocational trades and industry teacher.

She is also the creator of the P.E.R.C.E.P.T.I.O.N. Shift™, a framework designed to help education leaders change how CTE is positioned so that students choose it and communities believe in it. Her work challenges long-standing assumptions about college and career pathways and helps leaders align messaging, systems, and structures to reflect the true value of CTE.

Beyond her work in K–12 education, Dr. Prudhomme extends her impact through entrepreneurship and service. She is a REALTOR®, a Board Certified Credit Consultant, and the founder of a nonprofit credit education school dedicated to empowering young women through financial literacy. Her work connects education to economic mobility—helping individuals not only gain skills but also build the financial foundation needed for long-term success.

When we change how people see Career and Technical Education, we change what students choose—and ultimately, what becomes possible for their future.

BRING DR. PRUDHOMME TO YOUR DISTRICT

Keynotes • Workshops • Consulting

If this book resonated with you—if you recognized your district in these pages, your students in these stories, or yourself in these moments of clarity and challenge—the next step is a conversation.

Dr. Donna Prudhomme is available for keynote presentations, professional development workshops, and district consulting engagements. Her work is grounded in the same principles that transformed Career and Technical Education in Beaumont ISD, and she brings that same energy, conviction, and clarity to every room she enters.

KEYNOTE PRESENTATIONS

Dr. Prudhomme delivers powerful keynote addresses for CTE conferences, administrator summits, district leadership retreats, and community events. Her signature keynote—"We Don't Have a CTE Problem. We Have a Perception Problem"—brings the P.E.R.C.E.P.T.I.O.N. Shift™ framework to life through story, strategy, and a call to action that leaders carry long after they leave the room.

PROFESSIONAL DEVELOPMENT

Dr. Prudhomme offers half-day and full-day workshops designed for CTE directors, campus administrators, counselors, and teachers. Sessions are customized to your district's specific context and focused on practical strategies for shifting perception, increasing visibility, and aligning messaging across every level of your system.

DISTRICT CONSULTING

For districts ready to go deeper, Dr. Prudhomme offers consulting engagements to assess your current CTE narrative, identify gaps in perception and messaging, and develop a customized P.E.R.C.E.P.T.I.O.N. Shift™ implementation plan. Her approach is direct, practical, and grounded in what actually works because she has lived it.

To inquire about booking, speaking rates, and availability:

- www.drdonnaprudhomme.com
- speak@drdonnaprudhomme.com

The story was always enough.
It just needed the right audience to finally hear it.

—**Dr. Donna Prudhomme**

Made in the USA
Coppell, TX
23 June 2026

83353244R00116